Henry Adams

and the

American Experiment

David R. Contosta

Henry Adams

and the

American Experiment

Edited by Oscar Handlin

Little, Brown and Company · *Boston* · *Toronto*

LIBRARY OF CONGRESS CATALOG CARD NO. 80-81199

ISBN 0-316-154008

I   H   G   F   E   D   C   B   A

HAL

*Published simultaneously in Canada
by Little, Brown & Company (Canada) Limited*

PRINTED IN THE UNITED STATES OF AMERICA

Credits

The Education of Henry Adams, *by Henry Adams. Copyright, 1918 by the Massachusetts Historical Society. Copyright, 1946 by Charles Adams. Reprinted by permission of the publisher, Houghton Mifflin Company.*

Letters of Henry Adams: 1858–1891, *by Worthington Chauncy Ford. Copyright renewed 1958 by Emily E. F. Lowes. Reprinted by permission of the publisher, Houghton Mifflin Company.*

Letters of Henry Adams: 1892–1918, *by Worthington Chauncy Ford. Copyright © renewed 1966 by Emily E. F. Lowes. Reprinted by permission of the publisher, Houghton Mifflin Company.*

To my parents
Miles Richard Contosta
Betty Mowry Contosta

Editor's Preface

THE CHANGES through which the United States passed after the Civil War evoked buoyant optimism among some observers, distressed pessimism among others. For most Americans the continental expansion of the United States, its burgeoning industry, and the spurt of its influence overseas were the culmination of a process of progress that had begun centuries earlier. The Republic, such people believed, now approached the ordained manifest destiny of which earlier generations had only dreamed.

Others, however, regarded the same developments with dismay. The wealth of the newly rich and the poverty of the masses, the slums of the great cities and the barren farms alike seemed evidence of a ruthless materialism that disregarded past values and ideals. While the pessimists formed but a tiny minority of the population, their comments provided trenchant criticism of their society.

Henry Adams inherited both a political role and a pessimistic outlook. His father, his grandfather, and his great grandfather had played prominent parts in the early history of the United States, but each of them also took a bleak view of events. It was significant that neither John nor John Quincy Adams had gained a second term in office and that Charles Francis Adams had not been able to achieve the elective goals to which he aspired. All of them had cause to be critical.

Henry Adams had even more cause than they to be skeptical. Situated in a corner of the nation that steadily lost influence, he could not accept change with equanimity. Year by year he and his brothers dourly watched their country slip away from them. They regarded public service as a family obligation, yet politics seemed ever less likely to provide the means of fulfilling it.

Early on Henry Adams felt the need to make his mark. Self-conscious, he could not satisfy himself, for he lacked the faith that society would recognize his merit. Ability and connections opened to him a variety of careers, and he distinguished himself in each. Nonetheless, he could not settle down, not in Boston or Cambridge or Washington. Everywhere he would always be a stranger to the world about him. Unwilling to share the values that society adopted, he drifted apart, all the while seeking explanations for developments of which he disapproved. In the process he acquired the strategic perspective for incisive analysis of his country at a time of transition.

OSCAR HANDLIN

Contents

Henry Adams

and the

American Experiment

I
The Making of an Adams

ALL HIS LIFE Henry Adams (1838–1918) reflected on the meaning of the American experiment. The experiment was, ironically, European in origin, born of Renaissance longings for a better society. Humanist thinkers saw the New World as a place for people to begin again, a second Eden where men and women freed from the bondage of medieval tradition might make a fresh start. Such was the hope of Thomas More, who chose America as the scene for his *Utopia*. Seventeenth-century religious reformers also turned hopefully to this western wilderness. There Christianity, purged of its imperfections, would teach people to live in agreement with God's laws. William Penn accordingly launched his Holy Experiment on the banks of the Delaware, just as earlier in Boston the English Puritans had erected their City on a Hill, a beacon of truth for all to admire and emulate.

In the century that followed there were always some, the Founding Fathers among them, who kept the idea alive. Asserting the essential goodness of humanity, the more optimistic founders wished to prove that ordinary citizens could govern themselves in peace and prosperity. Once released from the influence of European corruption, the populace would demonstrate its inherent wisdom and morality.

These ideals continued to inspire and motivate Americans. The great domestic reform movements, as well as much of the country's foreign policy, were efforts to realize the founders' plans. At times the United States has vowed to remain aloof from Europe's quarrels, fearing the influences of the jaded Old World; just as often, however, it has wished to share its way of life with others. Both at home and abroad many Americans have felt a strong sense of mission. They have been determined to show the essential intelligence and morality of all people, believing that the result would raise the sum of human happiness.

From an early age Henry Adams wished to play a role in this mission. As it turned out, his participation was almost wholly cerebral. Rejecting an active political life, he became a journalist, historian, and man of letters. Yet family connections and personal charm gave him access to many politicians and high government officials. His comments upon their actions and upon nearly every facet of national life between the Civil War and World War I made him a most perceptive observer of the American experiment.

Adams, however, was much more than a commentator on his times. He was not content to record and criticize happenings of the day in isolation; he insisted on placing them in the context of larger forces. To Adams, past, present, and future were one thread, and he never ceased to look for mental spools about which to wrap it. His success in doing so made him something of a prophet and accounted for much of his continuing appeal.

As Adams grew older, his predictions about the country's future became increasingly pessimistic, although he never quite despaired altogether. Right before his death (which occurred during the last months of World War I) he had little faith that the United States could succeed in its mission. In many respects Adams anticipated that sense of disappointment and deflation so familiar in the 1920s. But Adams's times alone did not explain his deepening pessimism. The influences of his native New England and of his famous family were central factors in his disillusionment. Equally important were his personality and the varied experiences of a long life.

Born in Boston on February 16, 1838, Adams was marked for life by communal and familial habits. The circumstances of his childhood and youth greatly affected his interpretation of American character. Socially and economically the Adamses belonged to Boston's highest class. They were among the two or three dozen families of exalted social position from a population of approximately eighty-five thousand in 1840. Their status depended upon several factors: The family traced its New England ancestry back to the 1630s; it had produced two presidents of the United States; its members were renowned for their morality, intelligence, and public spirit; and they were among the wealthier inhabitants of the city. Wealth had come to the Adamses only recently as a result of the marriage between Henry's father, Charles Francis Adams, and Abigail Brooks, daughter of Peter Chardon Brooks, Boston's richest citizen. The Brookses, who had made their fortune in maritime commerce, also traced their lineage back to seventeenth-century New England.

The family of Charles Francis Adams lived on Beacon Hill, the favored location of elite families ever since authorities had decided to erect a new state house on the summit of the hill overlooking the Boston Common. From their residence at 57 Mount Vernon Street, in a house that Peter Chardon Brooks had purchased for them, the Adamses could see the gilded Bulfinch dome looming above the capitol. The dwelling itself was a four-story, red brick structure built in the early years of the nineteenth century and, like most of the other houses of the street, it shared a common wall with neighbors on either side.

Although the Adamses had a distaste for certain Boston traits, particularly the stiff social etiquette and the merchants' reputation for greed, the family shared most of the values and attitudes of so-called proper Bostonians. Proper Bostonians were proud of their families and of their contributions to city, state, and nation. They looked to elderly and departed members of the clan for standards, cherishing stories of their exemplary conduct and quoting their admonitions. Bostonians carefully preserved family papers and themselves wrote or commissioned others to write laudatory biographies of respected ancestors. Foreseeing the day when their heirs might look to them for guidance, they kept detailed diaries and preserved copies of their letters.

Proper Bostonians confined their social activities to a close circle and conducted themselves according to rigid customs. They expected their children to draw friends from this circle and eventually to choose a mate from within it. The Adamses were no exception. They also shared their class's reputation for bluntness. James Russell Lowell once said that the family had a "genius for saying even a gracious thing in an ungracious way."

Charles Francis Adams and his family long had abandoned orthodox Calvinism, but they retained part of the old Puritan belief that Boston constituted a latter-day City on a Hill. They regarded New England's way of life as superior to other areas of the country and believed that they had a duty to set moral and intellectual standards for the entire nation. Although not overly optimistic, they held that a steady application of reason and morality to human affairs could make the world a better place in which to live. This attitude found wide acceptance in Boston. Hence Bostonians with means often were generous in their support of public lectures, schools, hospitals, relief charities, and projects to beautify the city. In fact, such attitudes made Boston a center of reform. There were demands for better treatment of criminals and the insane and for greater women's rights. Others campaigned against alcoholism and prostitution. The more idealistic, many of them transcendentalists, endeavored to set up a utopian community at nearby Brook Farm. But the most vocal and most successful movement was the crusade against slavery. The majority of Bostonians opposed the agitation at first, especially the radical abolitionism of William Lloyd Garrison. Nevertheless, antislavery advocates grew in numbers and respectability.

In 1838 when Henry Adams was born, mass immigration had not yet destroyed the community's cultural and religious homogeneity, nor had rapid industrialization and urbanization produced a world that was utterly unamenable to the earlier Boston view of reality. Henry Adams was thus part of a community and a class sure of both its position and purpose in life.

Henry was the fourth of the Adams's six children: Louisa (b. 1831), John Quincy II (b. 1833), Charles Francis, Jr. (b. 1835), Mary (b. 1846), and Brooks (b. 1848). Neither Henry nor his siblings left a satisfactory record of their childhood relations. Henry may have looked up to his older brother Charles, to whom he turned for advice and approval in early adulthood. Brooks was ten years Henry's junior and the two were not close as children; in later years Henry recalled the shameful way he and the other boys had teased and bullied little Brooks. Louisa appears to have been a model of feminine beauty and charm for Henry. Of his sister Mary's and his brother John's early years he made no mention at all.

He was just as silent about his parents' lives during these childhood days. But after his father's death, he exclaimed that Charles Francis Adams was the most perfectly balanced, both intellectually and emotionally, of anyone in the family. Henry's mother was kindly, affectionate, and understanding, a complement to her more forbidding husband. The few extant letters from Henry to his mother reflect a warm and compassionate relationship.

Adams apparently believed that what passed between himself and the immediate family was not the concern of outsiders. Indeed, most proper Bostonians had a strong sense of family privacy; in reading their biographies or memoirs, one is led to believe that the subject had no intimate life whatever. Yet Adams realized his unquestionable debt to family influences. On the first page of the autobiographical *Education of Henry Adams,* he wrote that the family imprint was as strong as if he had been born a Jew in Jerusalem and had been circumcised by "his uncle the high priest." Following this tantalizing statement, however, Adams failed to supply a detailed description of how familial attitudes were transmitted to him. Yet he did suggest in the initial chapters of the *Education* and in other scattered remarks some outlines of the transmission.

Very early Henry became a private secretary to his father Charles Francis Adams. The elder Adams, having retired from active law practice and having for the time being shunned public office, spent much of his time between 1850 and 1858 editing the papers of his grandfather John Adams and writing a biography of the family patriarch. He enlisted Henry's help, installing a special writing table in the library where Henry read proof and performed other minor chores. Reading through his great-grandfather's own writings and through his father's biography of the man, Henry became very familiar with John Adams's character and philosophy of life.

A son of the Enlightenment, John Adams believed that there was a moral and intellectual order in the universe that all people, endowed at birth with conscience and reason, could discern. Mixed with this enlightened optimism were survivals from Adams's Puritan past, a strong sense of elitism and original sin, if only in secular garb. Although everyone possessed an innate ability to discover the good and the true, some inherited more potential than others. Yet even among the favored, life was a constant battle against sin and error. Those who best succeeded belonged to the natural aristocracy of wisdom and virtue and had a duty to lead their brethren. The family patriarch passed this philosophy on to his son John Quincy and he, to his son Charles Francis, and each expected his offspring to practice it throughout life. Unfortunately, the fathers were sometimes too hard on their children; two of John Quincy's sons broke under the pressure to succeed in the family mold. One committed suicide as a young man and the other died an early death from alcoholism and its complications.

The documents of John Adams's life also demonstrated to Henry his great-grandfather's constant habit of introspection and self-analysis, along with his persistent political independence. As a matter of conscience he refused to support the Hamiltonian wing of the Federalist party in its demands for war with France, a position that cost him a second presidential term.

Henry also received an early and practical education in politics. From his desk in the library he could listen to discussions between his father and his chief political associates, Charles Sumner and Richard Henry Dana. These talks added to Henry's understanding of the family's brand of independent politics. Like John Adams before him, Charles Francis Adams refused to follow any party line contrary to his best judgment. He had begun his political life as an Anti-Mason and subsequently became a Whig, a Conscience Whig, and a Free-Soiler. In 1848 the Free-Soilers had nominated him for vice-president on a ticket headed by Martin Van Buren. Later he became a Republican.

When Henry was twelve, his father gave him a chance to observe the political process at first hand during a trip to Washington. Charles Francis Adams wished to see his mother, who had settled permanently in the capital after her husband's death, and also wanted to discuss strategy with Free-Soil legislators. Henry was taken onto the floor of both House and Senate and there met the legislative giants of the day, Henry Clay, Daniel Webster, and John C. Calhoun. They were hard at work trying to save the Union from sectional strife in the aftermath of the Mexican War and succeeded in putting together the Compromise of 1850. Descendant of two presidents and son of a man with political promise, Henry Adams had a ringside seat to the making of history.

The trip to Washington was Henry's first contact with the South. The young New Englander was both enchanted and disgusted by what he saw. He loathed slavery more than ever upon seeing it up close, and he thought the southern landscape very untidy in comparison to the neat farmhouses and villages of Massachusetts. On the other hand, the casualness of the South and the personal warmth of southerners appealed to the boy who had grown up among the restraints both of family and community. The South attracted a side of him that was soon to rebel against the impositions of family, and it continued to do so for the rest of his life. He would one day make the nation's capital his home in part because of its southern flavor.

Another highlight in Henry's boyhood was the annual visit to grandfather John Quincy Adams. Every summer Charles Francis Adams and his brood moved to the family homestead in Quincy. Henry reveled in the months spent there, where he was free from the oppression and gloom of winter, from the grind of school, and from the formalities of Boston society. Alternating between Boston and Quincy gave Henry the sense of living two lives, each of which satisfied one side of his nature. Boston represented the part that wanted to conform to family standards and expectations; Quincy fed his resentment at being an Adams. As he explained in the *Education,* Boston and Quincy "were two hostile lives, and bred two separate natures. Winter was always the effort to live; summer was tropical license."

Although only ten miles from the center of Boston, Quincy had been another world to the Adamses since the time of great-grandfather John. He had practiced law in Boston, had lived in the city during various periods of his life, and had solicited the political support of Bostonians, but he always had looked upon his native Quincy (originally Brain-tree) as home. In his day the rural village, surrounded by rolling hills and lush farms, stood in stark contrast to the Boston world of business and finance to which he and most of his heirs never could accommodate themselves entirely. Both John and John Quincy Adams had returned to the family home to recoup after being defeated in a second bid for the presidency, and Charles Francis Adams would retire there too. They agreed with Jefferson that human virtue was best nurtured on the land. The family's base at Quincy also represented a rebelliousness in them all that would not let them reside comfortably in Boston. Henry's love for Quincy was thus another trait shared with the family.

The "old house" at Quincy that John Adams had pur-chased upon his return from England in 1788 was itself very different in mood and taste from nineteenth-century Boston. A rambling, two-story frame structure, heated by wood-burning fireplaces and lighted by candles or oil lamps, it boasted of no indoor plumbing. Its furnishings were Louis Quinze pieces that John and Abigail had brought back from Paris. Henry's house in Boston, on the other hand, con-tained more modern furniture and was complete with gas lights, an indoor bath, and central heating. For Henry the Quincy abode and its inhabitants were links to the eigh-teenth century. In future years it would become more and more removed from an increasingly industrialized Boston of brick and stone, although Quincy was eventually swal-lowed up by urban sprawl.

Visiting Quincy every summer, Henry grew fond of his grandmother Louisa Johnson Adams. She had been born in England and had lived much of her youth in Paris, and she never had shared her husband's passion for rural Quincy. Nor could the internationally minded woman accommodate herself to Puritan New England, and accordingly she settled in Washington after John Quincy's death. Henry sensed that she did not belong to Massachusetts. She wore, he remembered, an aura of eighteenth-century refinement and resembled a delicate "Romney portrait." He liked her for her own brand of resistance and refusal to conform to family preferences.

But his grandfather held the greatest personal attraction at Quincy. John Quincy Adams, like his father and his son, was a political maverick, insisting always upon pursuing the right as he saw it. While Federalist senator from Massachusetts, he voted for Jeffersonian measures he thought were in the national interest, including the acquisition of Louisiana and the embargo. In retaliation his Federalist backers refused him a second term. Even his acceptance of a seat in the U.S. House after losing the presidency to Andrew Jackson was a matter of conscience and duty. Family and friends had thought it degrading for an ex-president to re-enter the legislature, but he accepted because his neighbors had called him to serve. For seventeen years he stood by them, dying while still on the job. During his tenure in the House he had won wide admiration for his tenacious stand against a gag rule that forbade submission of antislavery petitions. He considered the gag rule a flagrant violation of First Amendment rights. Largely through his efforts the House finally repealed the obnoxious rule.

Since congressional sessions then began in early December and commonly broke up in the spring, John Quincy Adams spent a good part of each year at home. Henry must have known something of his grandfather's renown. To the child, however, he was mostly a kind and determined old man who sat in the library going over his affairs and keeping track of his conscience in regular diary entries. As his grandfather sat at the desk, Henry liked to poke into drawers and derange the president's papers. He also enjoyed collecting the best fruits of the orchard and presenting them to the old man, who used their seeds to start new trees.

Gentle though he was, the grandfather did not let Henry shirk his duties. For example, the family decided one year that Henry would attend classes at the local school, even though it was summer. Unwilling to have his paradise disrupted, Henry refused to go one morning. When John Quincy discovered what was afoot, the septuagenarian climbed down from his library, took the boy firmly by the hand, and walked with him in the hot morning sun the one mile to school. He did not utter a word the whole way, but the actions of the elderly and determined gentleman were worth more than a stern lecture or physical punishment. His grandson would have to learn that education was part of the moral and intellectual order.

Henry obtained most of his schooling in Boston. His studies followed a course much like that of others in his social class. He began at the small primary school just a few doors from his parents' Mount Vernon Street house. After that he attended the intermediate school of David B. Tower. He was supposed to continue at the Boston Latin School; but because Charles Francis Adams had heard bad reports about the headmaster, he went instead to E. S. Dixwell's for college preparation. Henry left no account of his studies there, but the principal aim of the school was to drill the students in Latin and Greek as well as in mathematics and English composition. He also said little about social life at school, simply stating in the *Education* that he enjoyed snowball battles on the Boston Common.

Sundays the pattern of school, study, and play was interrupted by church services in both morning and afternoon. The Adamses belonged to the First Boston Church, one of many congregations that embraced Unitarianism a generation earlier. In the pulpit stood Henry's maternal uncle Nathaniel L. Frothingham. Henry and his brother Charles later remembered how much they had detested the long sermons and how much they had hated Sundays in general. From midweek on they dreaded its coming and reveled in Monday morning as a release from Sabbath gloom.

Even though Henry did not listen to most of the sermons,

the religious ideas they promulgated were important influences in his life. The Unitarian philosophy was nearly identical to the eighteenth-century facets of Adams family thought. American Unitarianism was born of the Enlightenment. Its clergy and laity questioned various tenets of orthodox Christianity, chiefly the doctrine of the Trinity, the sect taking its name from an insistence upon the unity of the Godhead. In general, they refused to stand upon dogma of any kind and shared with the *philosophes* of the eighteenth century a belief in individual conscience and religious toleration. They further shared the Enlightenment's belief in a moral and rational world order. It was the duty of Unitarians to apply in daily life those laws that reason and conscience revealed. The faithful also maintained that such laws were discernible in Scripture, once they had discarded those passages that were obviously unreasonable or purely reflections of biblical culture. In the last analysis, Unitarians asserted that there was no conflict between reason and revelation. These ideas accorded closely with the Adamses' world view, although the family added a strong dose of Puritan pessimism.

As adults Henry and his brothers abandoned the religious faith of childhood and became agnostics, a position that did not demand subscription to any doctrine or creed. Nevertheless, in secular form Adams clung to the Unitarian principles of both church and home. And when he entered college in the fall of 1854, he discovered that Harvard upheld an essentially identical world view.

In attending Harvard Adams once again did what was expected of him, for elite Bostonians thought it to be the only college in the country worthy of consideration. Generation after generation had sent their sons to and had lavished gifts upon the learned institution just across the Charles River. Harvard had been an Adams tradition since John had graduated in 1755. John Quincy had taught rhetoric there during a lull in his public career and later had served on the Board of Overseers. Charles Francis Adams likewise served on the board, and Henry's uncle Edward Everett had been president for several years.

The core of Harvard's curriculum at that time included Greek, Latin, mathematics, philosophy, rhetoric, written composition, and religious instruction. A few scientific courses had appeared on the required list, and students could take several electives. The modern languages also had risen in importance, although not at the expense of the classics. Many of Adams's courses reinforced the values of church and home. The faculty were, for the most part, New Englanders and Unitarians; James Walker, the president, was an ordained Unitarian minister, as were several professors. Walker's compulsory series of religious lectures presented the "argument from design." The president began by indicating the many evidences of structure in creation, asserting that such order must be the work of an intelligent Creator. In his ethics class, which Adams also attended, Walker applied the argument to human behavior. The Divine Mind had willed every object for a specific purpose discernible in its nature. Man's end was determined by conscience and reason, characteristics that differentiated him from the rest of creation. Refusal to behave in a moral and rational manner was to deny one's humanity and to flout the will of God and nature. John Adams would have agreed readily.

Henry confronted the design argument again in political economy, a course given by philosopher Francis Bowen, who treated the subject as a branch of ethics. According to Bowen, the most significant aspect of human economic behavior was a desire to buy cheaply and sell dearly. On the surface such behavior would seem to produce great evil. But Bowen, echoing Adam Smith, assured Adams and his classmates that God made economic selfishness work for the good. A desire for the best deal in the marketplace ensured that labor, resources, capital, and finished products would end up where most needed. Behind human selfishness was a benign law of nature.

In a course on government and the American Constitution, Henry W. Torrey similarly took an ethical approach. Good government rested upon certain principles, among them the need for leadership by the more moral and intelligent members of society. Torrey also believed, in agreement with John Adams, that even the best persons were tempted to abuse power. Hence all political authority had to be divided and checked. These devices also guaranteed that the majority would not have their way without sufficient contemplation and delay, thereby precluding hasty and ill-advised action.

Adams even heard the familiar assertion of universal order, law, and purpose in a group of lectures by Louis Agassiz entitled "The Glacial Theory and Paleontology." A geologist and zoologist of international renown, Agassiz had been the first to put forth a systematic theory explaining the effects of glaciers upon the earth's crust and life forms. He had founded his conclusions on careful research, but he never ceased believing that the hand of God lay behind the glaciers, calling them "God's great plows." To the end of his life Agassiz insisted that nature revealed a divine scheme, so much so that he became the nation's most outspoken opponent of Darwinian evolution. Years later, when Adams began to have doubts about evolution, Professor Agassiz's lectures would take on new meaning.

Agassiz as well as Adams's other professors expected students to recite what they had heard and read. Harvard did little to encourage curiosity or originality; if students developed intellectual imagination, it was in spite of the college's methods of instruction. Adams recognized these faults, and a dozen years later he was willing to return to Harvard as a teacher and to participate in a thorough reform of the institution.

Harvard was not all study though, and Adams was in no sense an academic drudge. He made friends easily, accompanying them to taverns, plays, and sporting events, and on occasion getting drunk with the others. He spent many evenings chatting with friends or reading novels that had nothing to do with his studies. In winter he liked to ice-skate, and in better weather he enjoyed hiking. Adams participated, too, in more organized extracurricular activities. The prestigious Hasty Pudding Club elected him a member in 1856, and he took part in several plays. He also was a member of the Institute of 1770 and contributed regularly to the *Harvard Magazine*. This work proved to be the beginning of his journalistic career, and *Harvard Magazine* was one of many vehicles which he would use to criticize the American people and their experiment. The moralistic tone that he took in several of the *Magazine* articles anticipated a similar note in his mature writings.

This tone was particularly evident in two pieces. In "Cap and Bells" (April 1858) he took fellow students to task for their haughtiness as college men, for their displays of superficial knowledge, and for a variety of other faults. "College Politics" (May 1857) attacked Greek letter societies as snobbish, hypocritical in their protestations of brotherhood, and destructive of college unity. He urged them to combine into several large associations resembling urban gentlemen's clubs. Students then would have a wider circle of acquaintances; they could forget their silly claims of exclusiveness; they might benefit from pooling their financial and intellectual resources. A concluding paragraph warned the fraternities, "You must soon virtually decide on the part you are to take. For the sake of good morals, and especially honesty and fairness; . . . for the sake of our successors; and, finally, for your own sakes, and your reputations as our foremost men, — we hope that your decision will be wise."

The high point of Adams's college days was being chosen Class Day Orator. His speech, delivered June 25, 1858, exhibited the same moral earnestness as his articles. Small in stature even for an Adams, standing 5 feet 3 inches and weighing only 125 pounds, the brown-haired, brown-eyed young man warned his peers to avoid the increasing materialism and commercialism of their age. He hoped they would remember the ideals of their professors and college, and he admonished them to "put their whole faith in those great truths, to the advancement of which Omnipotence itself has not refused its aid." Adams had learned his lessons well. If he showed little originality, he must have pleased faculty and parents by parroting their moral certainties.

A month after the Class Day celebration Henry Adams received his Harvard degree. Now he faced the prospect of choosing a career. His education had given him a broad background but did not prepare him for any particular field. Many of his classmates, who had received the same education, were intent upon careers in the ministry, law, medicine, commerce, literature, or science. Adams, however, did not know what to do with his life — for that matter, he never really made up his mind. His quandary was compounded by the knowledge that his family expected much from him. In this state of indecision he proposed to take a grand tour of Europe, as was the custom of many upper-class young men. For Adams the grand tour was a moratorium from decision, permitting him to delay the choice of a career.

As an Adams, such a release was not easy to arrange. Henry's own Puritan conscience balked at the thought of wandering aimlessly around Europe. He also knew that Charles Francis Adams would meet the proposal coldly. Accordingly, Henry determined to study law while abroad, with the thought of continuing legal studies after he returned. His father, grandfather, and great-grandfather all had entered law, and it had provided a modest living as well as a springboard to more exalted accomplishments. He succeeded in selling these plans to his father. He would study law at the University of Berlin, which had a worldwide reputation in the legal field. It may have been Henry's choice of Berlin that helped to convince his father the young man knew what he was doing.

Adams left New York at the end of September 1858 and arrived in Liverpool eleven days later after a grievous bout of seasickness, an affliction that would bother him the rest of his life. From England he proceeded to Berlin via Hanover. His first lectures at the university convinced him that his college German was inadequate; he could not understand a word. Advice from an American acquaintance in the city sent him to a secondary school, where he enrolled in the hopes of improving his language skills. For the next three months the twenty-three-year-old Adams sat in class with boys six or eight years his junior.

Henry suspected that Charles Francis Adams would be unhappy about his decision. Wishing to please his father, he could not help feeling a sense of failure and guilt. Because he was reluctant to unburden himself to the elder Adams — fearing that his reaction would be a stream of admonitions about duty and perseverence — Henry turned to brother Charles, who was now reading law in Boston and seemed self-assured. Charles was generally sympathetic and offered constructive suggestions. When Henry wrote that he thought himself unfit for a legal career, Charles proposed a literary life instead, as his *Harvard Magazine* articles had shown promise. Henry rejected the idea, believing that it was not commensurate with his larger ambitions. He also complained of their father's outspoken disapproval. Wounded by these scoldings, Henry defended himself to Charles, saying, "I'm doing my best to do well here, God knows, and it's excessively unpleasant to be told without any why or wherefore that I'm becoming a damned fool." Charles tried to intercede for his brother at home. Yet there were times when Henry resented Charles's advice as much as his father's.

Henry's letters revealed that he was extremely sensitive

to criticism and that he felt keenly the pressure to succeed. Despite his desire to please those at home, he made little effort to resume his legal studies. For a time he tried reading a bit of law on his own, but he was bored by law and eventually dropped it altogether. He spent the next year and a half traveling in the company of several college friends who also had taken the grand tour following graduation.

Throughout Adams's sojourn the continent was embroiled in the wars of Italian liberation and unification. While planning a trip to Italy in the spring of 1860, he struck upon the idea of recording his impressions of events in a series of letters to some American newspaper. He discussed the project with Charles, who arranged for publication in the Boston *Courier*. The letters began to appear on April 30. In these letters Henry demonstrated again his abilities as a writer. They also revealed much about his political and social prejudices. By using family connections, he arranged a meeting with Garibaldi, who had just captured Sicily. Mentioning that Europeans called Garibaldi the Washington of Italy, he reported that he felt none of that respect due the American original. There the Italian leader stood, Adams related to his readers, in his red shirt (the symbol and uniform of his army), looking like a common American fireman. He had "no mark of authority" that the correspondent could see. The noble, dignified Washington would have been aghast at the thought of "invading a foreign kingdom on his own hook, in a fireman's shirt!" In Adams's opinion Garibaldi was not the proper sort to lead a revolution. Nor did any of the Italian leaders appear suitable. He wondered why the better class of people did not step forth to guide the revolution along safe and intelligent paths, as America's enlightened founders had done.

As summer waned, Adams's two years in Europe came to an end and he sailed for home. He had seen a good deal of western Europe, had improved his German, and had gained experience as a writer. But at the time he could not appreciate his adventures, and he felt sharply his failure with the law. Knowing that he was no closer to a career than before, he realized that he had disappointed his father and family.

The young man returning from the Continent was an Adams through and through. He shared the family's political, social, and intellectual prejudices; he had taken up familial habits of introspection and self-castigation; he had begun to develop a critical attitude toward persons and institutions around him. He also arrived home in a crisis of identity, wishing to be an Adams and at the same time resenting it. The stage was set for his participation in and his reflections upon the American experiment. In the months immediately ahead the country would confront its greatest challenge since 1787, and Henry Adams would play a minor role in seeing it to safety.

II

Crisis

HENRY REACHED HOME in October 1860 to find
the Federal Union, a cornerstone of the founders' design,
on the verge of disintegration. Various factors had led to
the impasse: the agitation of abolitionists; a growing diver-
gence between ways of life in North and South; disputes
over the extension of slavery into the territories. But the
Republican nomination of Abraham Lincoln for the presidency brought matters to a head. Adamantly opposing the
spread of slavery, Lincoln filled southerners with alarm.
South Carolina threatened to secede if he were elected.

During his two years abroad, Henry had kept abreast of
the growing crisis through newspapers and letters from
home. He had been particularly interested in the political
response to events because of his father's election to the
U.S. House in the fall of 1858. Returning home he found
Charles Francis Adams at the height of his campaign for
reelection and at the peak of his exertions on behalf of
Lincoln.

Although the elder Adams shared Lincoln's opposition
to the spread of slavery, he shuddered at the thought of
disunion. Without firm union and effective central government, regional jealousies would diminish economic welfare

and endanger liberty. Tariff barriers would arise among the states, and local demagogues would flourish unchecked. The nation might return to the days of Shays' Rebellion or worse. Secession would prove, too, that foreign critics had been right all along in their doubts about the New World's superiority. Americans would show themselves no more able to escape regional strife than their European brethren if they failed to end the iniquity of slavery in an intelligent and peaceful manner. They would prove to be as irrational and immoral as the peoples from whom they had sprung.

Regardless of the impending storm, Henry decided that he owed the law one more chance and began reading in the Boston firm of Judge Horace Gray. But his second attempt at legal education did not last long. Charles Francis Adams, victorious in his bid for reelection, asked his son to go to Washington as private secretary. Charles Francis seemed willing to accept Henry's distaste for the law and probably wished to provide a temporary alternative. In formally designating Henry his secretary, he also appeared to be making him heir to the family's public fortunes.

Henry accepted the family apprenticeship with foreboding, earnestly desiring to prove himself worthy of his illustrious ancestors. He was to serve as private secretary for eight years, spending only a few months of it in Washington, after which President Lincoln made Charles Francis Adams minister to Great Britain. During these years Henry not only received training in the family's political and diplomatic vocations but also did his own small part to save the Union. He also worked out a plan for helping to guide the American experiment once peace returned. Unfortunately, it was not a time free from self-deprecation and self-doubt. Henry continued to fear that he was incapable of meeting family expectations and suffered from an ongoing identity crisis, which he resolved for the time being only by throwing himself into his immediate duties and postwar calculations.

The private secretary began his job in December 1860.

When he and his father arrived in Washington, South Carolina already had called a convention to consider secession, and several more southern states were about to follow suit. Since Lincoln did not take office until March 4 and since the lame duck Buchanan was virtually powerless, it was up to Congress to keep the peace until inauguration day.

Congressman Adams belonged to the moderate wing of the Republican party, headed by Senator William H. Seward of New York. They opposed the expansion of slavery but also cherished the Union. Their goal was to effect a compromise between North and South, preventing secession and war; meanwhile they continued to oppose the spread of slavery and to hope for its gradual and peaceful extinction. In opposition to the moderates was an increasingly radical group led by Senator Charles Sumner of Massachusetts. Sumner, long a vehement enemy of slavery, was ready to risk disunion in order to extirpate it. Charles Francis Adams's position was particularly difficult since he and Sumner were old friends and political allies.

Congressman Adams received an appointment to the House Committee of Thirty-Three to formulate a legislative and constitutional compromise between the conflicting sections. (The Senate created a similar Committee of Thirteen.) Well-schooled in the virtues of moderation, Henry shared his father's views and wished to lend support. And because of the favorable reception of his *Courier* letters, he decided to use his pen to uphold the congressman's positions. With this end in mind, he secured appointment as Washington correspondent for the Boston *Advertiser,* the most important Republican newspaper in the state. Its editor, Charles Hale, one of Charles Francis Adams's backers as well as family friend, agreed to withhold Henry's name so as not to compromise the elder Adams.

Henry's initial letters to the *Advertiser,* the first dated December 7, reiterated his father's and Senator Seward's early suspicions that the secessionists were bluffing in order to wring concessions from the federal government. The two legislators preferred to believe that the majority of southerners supported the Union and would refuse to break away; once the patriots of the South had made themselves heard, the secessionists would back down. South Carolina's defection and the conventions held in other states, however, made Adams and Seward change their minds, and they actively sought compromise. Adams accordingly seconded the proposal of Maryland Congressman Winter Davis to admit New Mexico as a slave state in the hopes that this action would pacify the South. By the end of December Henry reflected the shift in strategy, praising Davis and defending moderate compromises. Congressman Adams strongly disapproved of slavery, his son wrote, but refused to risk violence and social disorder until all peaceful alternatives had been explored.

The end of January saw seven more states secede, and war seemed imminent. In desperation House and Senate entertained several more compromises, all of which Henry extolled to his readers. None of them saved the peace in the end, but the debates bought time until Lincoln could take office. Henry's part in the stalling action was small; still, his columns had a salutary effect on public opinion in Massachusetts. They convinced editor Hale to embrace the moderate position and pacified a portion of Charles Francis Adams's more radical constituency.

The calm and cautious mood of the letters did not mean that Henry was without private emotions. In his continuing correspondence with brother Charles, he blasted the South for not sharing the reason and moderation of the best New England tradition. He wrote in January 1861 that the secessionists were plain mad; it was the North's duty to "lock them up till they become sane." He wanted "to educate, humanize and refine them." For the time being he ignored those elements of southern life that had appealed to him a dozen years before. Nevertheless, he did not forget that his own section of the country bore some of the blame. He berated Sumner's extremism and continuously lauded their father's more sensible efforts at peace.

Meanwhile, Charles Francis Adams received an important diplomatic post; on March 19, 1861, the president designated him minister to Great Britain. In typical Adams fashion the new minister showed no elation at the assignment, worrying instead if he were fit for the duty thrust upon him. In his diary Charles, Jr., wrote of the family's consternation: "My mother at once fell into tears and deep agitation; foreseeing all sorts of evil consequences, and absolutely refusing to be comforted; while my father looked dismayed."

Henry agreed to continue as private secretary and before leaving the country offered to serve as the *New York Times'* London correspondent. Editor Henry Raymond, whom he had met while covering Washington for the *Advertiser,* promised to keep his reports anonymous. It was more important than ever not to be discovered, for revelation might mean the end of his father's diplomatic career. Henry knew better than to tell even his father, certain that he would forbid the assignment in the name of propriety and caution.

On May 1 Charles Francis Adams and his wife with three of their children, Henry, Brooks, and Mary, left for England. The United States had failed to avert secession and war, and it remained to be seen if the Union could be restored. Both the minister and his son knew that their country faced the greatest test since the Revolution. As they steamed across the Atlantic, they must have thought of John Adams's mission to Europe during the darkest days of the War of Independence. His job to win the support of the world's great powers was now his grandson's assignment. Charles Francis had to convince the British to refrain in any way from aiding the Confederacy. Success with Great Britain would doubtless bring the other countries into line. Failure might bring war between the United States and Britain and any country that likewise helped the rebels. With civil war at home, foreign conflict would surely mean disaster.

When the Adamses reached Liverpool on May 13 they learned to their consternation that Queen Victoria had just issued a Proclamation of Neutrality. The new minister's initial response was entirely negative. He thought it an unfriendly act, for it gave southerners the status of an independent power and greatly strengthened their morale. However, the minister and his secretary soon grasped the political factors behind neutrality and learned to use them advantageously.

Henry was learning that domestic affairs were inseparable from a country's foreign policy. In the pages of the *New York Times* he endeavored to explain this to his public and to solicit their patience with Great Britain. In addition, he tried to show them why the United States must cultivate those Britons who leaned toward the Union cause. Most of all, he worked to allay American anger over the Queen's proclamation. When on May 21 his father received Secretary of State Seward's preposterous threats of war against Britain and France, Henry redoubled his efforts to calm fellow citizens. Continuing with his father to believe that coolness and reason were the foundations of wise policy, he worked hard to nurture a judicious and reflective climate at home.

In a letter to the *Times* on June 22, 1861, Henry explained the relationships between domestic and foreign policy in Britain. Confusion over the American conflict and lack of party discipline in Parliament made it difficult for Prime Minister Palmerston to fashion a clear-cut policy for or against the Union and resulted in the neutrality proclamation. On November 2 he urged Americans to look with favor upon Palmerston and the Whig party because the collapse of his government would return the Tories, landed aristocrats who tended to side with the South.

Henry maintained that the North's best friends in Britain were the liberals. Although they composed no formal party, vocal independents like John Bright and Richard Cobden spoke for the cause in the House of Commons. Other liberals like John Stuart Mill showed their support in influential periodicals such as the *Westminster Review*. For decades they had attacked slavery and had applauded the advance of democratic institutions around the world. They feared that liberalism would suffer a tragic setback if the North lost. In order to hold their support, Henry urged the United States to announce that the war was in part a crusade against slavery. An emancipation proclamation would help the American minister in London, who was straining every nerve to cultivate friends for the Union. A year and a half later Lincoln would issue just such a proclamation, anticipating the declaration's salutary effect on world opinion.

Another of Henry's concerns was the pressure that the British textile industry might bring against the government. Cotton manufacturers depended on the South for eighty percent of their raw fiber; with the supply cut by the northern blockade, it was conceivable that they would demand intervention. Adams hoped that "principle will overbalance the mere matter of money-making." In Britain, as in America, morality coupled with reason and moderation was the guiding principle.

A personal visit to Manchester, the center of the cotton industry, enabled him to meet factory owners, newspapermen, and public officials and to tour factories. The written report, too long for the usual column allotted in the *New York Times,* appeared in the Boston *Courier* under the title "Diary of a visit to Manchester." Henry found a heartening idealism among textile workers who hated slavery and sided with the North. Most of the middle class owners shared their employees' sentiments. In any case, Adams saw little reason to fear that textile interests would demand armed resistance to the blockade of southern ports. Unemployment in Manchester was largely due to overproduction. Further, the supply of raw cotton in the city was adequate because manufacturers had anticipated the shortage. When they ran out of the southern staple, they were sure to receive quantities of Indian and Egyptian fiber, which experts deemed as suitable as the American variety. Henry believed that these realities would calm Union fears of British interference.

In the account of his visit to Manchester Adams also included a few paragraphs on Manchester social life, which he found friendlier and more generous than London's. Through a misunderstanding, the *Courier* revealed Henry's authorship of the article, and the British press chided his inability to appreciate refined London society. Henry was utterly humiliated and turned to Charles for consolation, writing, "To my immense astonishment and dismay I found myself this morning sarsed through a whole column of the [London] Times, and am laughed at by all England." Adams was frightened and annoyed. He worried that knowledge of his authorship might lead to exposure as *New York Times* correspondent, and he quickly resigned from the job.

Henry's overreaction to the results of his Manchester article suggests that he was having a difficult time emotionally. He continued to sense the family pressure to succeed and considered his contribution to the war as insignificant. Copying dispatches for his father and writing a weekly newspaper column seemed as nothing in comparison to the sacrifices of young men on the battlefield. While he had sat at his desk in London, a third of his Harvard classmates had enlisted in the war, and even Charles, Jr., had obtained a commission.

As early as June 1861, Henry was apologizing to his brother for his civilian status, contending that their father needed him at the legation and claiming that he was unfit for military service. By August he had changed his mind:

He decided that the minister did not really require him and asked Charles to find him a commission. His brother advised him to stay put. Henry finally gave up on the army, but he still was unhappy with himself. December found him thoroughly depressed; he wrote to Charles, "For my own part I am tired of this life. Every attempt I have made to be of use has failed more or less completely." Charles upbraided him for his pessimism, urging him to leave the legation and strike out on his own. Then he could concentrate on journalism with no worries about exposure. Admitting that his state of mind was morbid and unhealthy, Henry rejoined, "I've disappointed myself, and experience the curious sensation of discovering myself to be a humbug." Later letters showed that the dark moods colored his view of the world at large. The South, he feared, would win, and everything wicked and selfish in American life would triumph. And this would not be the last time that his state of mind distorted his perceptions of the American experiment.

Henry was a victim of the family's traditional pessimism, yet he was also in the grip of a still unresolved personal crisis. Proud of being an Adams and grateful for the advantages the family had given him, he doubted he could live up to its high standards. At the same time he could not break away and carve out a vocation for himself. Succeeding in a field outside traditional family occupations might have freed him from comparing himself to other members of the clan and given him a clearer sense of purpose.

As the Adamses became better established in London and made friends, they began to enjoy a busy social life, which helped take Henry's mind away from personal troubles. At an endless procession of breakfasts, luncheons, teas, dinners, and balls, he met some of the most notable Britons, at least those who belonged to the liberal camp. There was the aging Charles Dickens, completing his last full novel *Our Mutual Friend,* while undermining his health through excessive work and play. Other literary lights in the Adams's circle included Algernon Swinburne, Robert Browning, and Leslie Stephen. Among political acquaintances were John Bright and Richard Cobden, both foes of slavery and warm friends of the Union. Rounding out the list were novelist and economist Harriet Martineau and scientific evangel Thomas Henry Huxley. None became close friends, but Henry could claim a sense of intimacy with Britain's greatest writers and thinkers.

He came to know other figures in the liberal ranks much better. The most engaging intellectually was Sir Charles Lyell, an accomplished geologist and a supporter of evolution. Also befriending Adams were two men who later helped him publish in the British press, Francis T. Palgrave and Richard Monckton Milnes. The closest of these friends, however, were James Milnes Gaskell and his son Charles, who was Henry's age. A member of Parliament, the elder Gaskell resided with his family in a ruined medieval abbey at Wenlock in Yorkshire. Adams and the son found they were kindred spirits, and they would remain devoted until death.

Besides an active social life, several diplomatic crises further occupied Henry: the American seizure of two Confederate envoys from a British vessel and the construction of ships for the South in British shipyards. But what lifted his spirits most were the forging of postwar plans and extensive reading, much of it linked to these plans. Well before the war ended Adams began to think about peacetime. He was concerned with the broader questions of morality and reason: Disunion had occurred because the American people and their leaders had strayed from the paths of wisdom and virtue. The country needed enlightened direction to restore those eternal verities espoused by John Adams a century earlier. Henry had in mind an elite group with background and training similar to his own, and to brother Charles he wrote, "We want a national set of young men like ourselves or better, to start new influences not only in politics, but in literature, in law, in society, and throughout the whole social organism of the country."

Henry found reinforcement for his ideas in the writings of Alexis de Tocqueville, John Stuart Mill, and Auguste Comte. Tocqueville's *Democracy in America* clearly supported his own and his family's belief in talented leaders. Tocqueville asserted that the wise and virtuous must counter those forces in democracies leading to mass mediocrity and the "tyranny of the majority." Mediocrity resulted from democratic insistence upon equality, a factor that caused many Americans to regard the thoughts of all people as equally acceptable. Some even believed the opinions of common citizens superior to those arrived at through cultivated reflection, a manifestation of democracy's faith in the morality and wisdom of majority rule. Unfortunately, there was no guarantee that the majority was either wise or virtuous; further, the majority was likely to intimidate anyone who did not agree with its deliberations and decisions. Like John Adams and John Quincy Adams, Tocqueville did not repudiate democracy, but he asserted that its dangerous aspects had to be curbed by an aristocracy of the wise and just. The Frenchman observed such a check at work when he visited New England. There the Puritan heritage preserved a respect for intelligence, ability, and education. If only the entire nation could share the discretion of New England, the democratic experiment would surely succeed.

But by the time Henry Adams reached adulthood, deference to one's betters had nearly disappeared in New England, too many citizens having adopted the Jacksonian creed. Old Hickory and his followers had taken advantage of universal male suffrage, popular selection of presidential electors, and grass roots party organizations. Expressing their faith in the commonality, Jacksonians appealed to the now-sovereign masses, arguing that anyone could enter pub-

lic office and attacking the concept of a professional and
permanent civil service. Career bureaucrats, they charged,
held privileged positions and were unresponsive to voters.
And although Jackson himself did not replace a large per-
centage of officeholders, he fired enough of them to establish a dangerous precedent. Government was to suffer from
the spoils system throughout the nineteenth century.

The Adamses did not look kindly upon Jacksonian Democracy with its faith in the common people and its
contempt for enlightened public servants. Furthermore,
Andrew Jackson had defeated John Quincy Adams in his
second run for the White House, and to the Adamses Jackson's victory demonstrated that honesty, morality, and education had lost to the forces of demagoguery, ignorance, and
corruption. The American people, it appeared, had no use
for the Adamses or their class.

The writings of John Stuart Mill, however, convinced
Henry that there was still hope for the gentleman in politics. He read Mill's *Consideration on Representative Government* shortly after he arrived in England. Mill agreed
with Tocqueville that the democratic masses needed the
guidance of a moral and intelligent elite. In this way alone
could government balance the interests of the many with
the abilities of the few. His confidence rested upon the universal need for valid information. Since individuals, from
the humblest to the most able, could not investigate every
question for themselves, they had to trust those they considered more knowledgeable. Politics was no exception;
voters and politicians had to have accurate and reliable
facts. It was the duty of the upright, the intelligent, and
the educated (the "informed" Mill called them) to make
their knowledge and judgments available.

An informed elite could function effectively only in a
free society. Free access to education and careers permitted
the talented person to rise to the elite classes regardless of
background. Such stands were consistent with the overall

laissez-faire position that Mill shared with nineteenth-century liberals. Free competition, whether in goods or ideas, would ensure truth, justice, and prosperity. Adams later repudiated much of Mill's liberal orthodoxy, but for the time being he took solace in the Englishman's political speculations. A free society, Mill assured him, did not necessarily condemn itself to mediocrity and majority tyranny, not if the capable influenced those who looked to them for guidance. No wonder Henry exclaimed to Charles that Mill, his "high priest," had shown that "democracy is still capable of rewarding a conscientious servant."

Auguste Comte, introduced to Henry through Mill's essay, "Auguste Comte and Positivism," was also encouraging. Comte explained that society had passed through two stages of intellectual development and was about to enter a third. Comte's first epoch, called the theological stage, had lasted in Europe until about 1500. During it people had sought religious explanations for their world. The second stage began when advanced thinkers started to treat the world in metaphysical terms. Objects behaved as they did because of natural laws or inherent propensities. The metaphysician was willing to admit that some sort of First Cause or Prime Mover lay behind these laws and propensities, but he denied the existence of a personal God. Most of the celebrated minds of the seventeenth and eighteenth centuries, including Isaac Newton and Thomas Jefferson, were basically metaphysical in their approach to reality. The nineteenth century then ushered in the third, or positive, stage of human thought. The positivist refused to look for explanations beyond observable phenomena; a person could trust only what the senses revealed about the physical, tangible world.

Comte believed that positivism was the only sure road to truth. Not until people abandoned religious and metaphysical perspectives would they escape from ignorance and realize the just and prosperous society. Eventually all would embrace the positive view; as people learned more about themselves and their world, the advantages of empirical knowledge would gain universal acceptance. An intelligent elite could accelerate the inevitable and, once the positive society emerged, would become the governing class, for only the informed could appreciate the intricacies of a world grounded in positive knowledge. Traditional government would give way to committees of scientific experts.

Adams did not accept Comte's thoroughgoing materialism, remaining an idealist at heart and continuing to accept certain moral and rational principles beyond the purely physical. His education and upbringing had stressed the reality of ideals, and he was only imperfectly aware of the contradiction between positivism and his own world view. But whatever the ultimate implications of a positive society, Adams was hopeful of finding a position in the postwar world from which he might help lead the American people. Upon returning to the United States in the summer of 1868, his father's mission at an end, he was determined to make himself an agent of informed opinion. His experiences as a journalist convinced him that the press held the best possibilities. Henry thus completed his years abroad with a sense of accomplishment and purpose. His father had kept Britain neutral throughout the war. By copying dispatches, assisting with social affairs, and discussing diplomatic plans, Henry had been a great help to the minister. In addition, he knew his columns in the *New York Times* had had a healthy effect on public opinion. Thus Henry returned to America with a modicum of confidence.

III

Mugwump Reformer

AFTER EIGHT YEARS in England, Charles Francis Adams and family arrived in New York City on July 7, 1868. Forty years later Henry remembered how they felt as they made their way into the government tugboat. "Had they been Tyrian traders of the year B.C. 1000, landing from a galley fresh from Gibraltar, they could hardly have been stranger on the shore of a world, so changed from what it had been ten years before." Adams exaggerated for literary effect the degree to which the country had changed in their absence. Yet it was true that the emergencies of 1861 had been replaced by a new set of problems, most of them resulting from the war. The economy of a prostrate South demanded restoration; seceded states must participate again in national government; ex-slaves required aid and protection in order to enter the mainstream of American life. With the Union restored, were states' rights a dead issue? If not, what was to be the new relationship between national and local government?

Central authority itself had suffered much change and stress during the conflict. Because of wartime emergency, national government had grown in functions and authority, giving rise to quarrels between the president and Congress over the proper balance of power. The impeachment and near conviction of Andrew Johnson was only the most dramatic episode in their tug of war. The means employed to finance the bloodshed also left an unsettling legacy. Congress had to decide whether to lower or to abolish wartime taxes, whether to return to a metallic currency, whether to retire the debt quickly or slowly.

Massive public spending during the war had stimulated the private sector. Some businessmen and industrialists had grown rich during the conflict, amassing enough capital to impel them to greater wealth afterwards. Andrew Carnegie, John D. Rockefeller, and other entrepreneurs were in positions at war's end to launch giant enterprises, the likes of which the world had never seen. Soon there would be calls for big government and big labor to serve as counterpoises to big business. In order to superintend the trusts, government would need batteries of experts and career bureaucrats. But political parties opposed the advent of a large and professional civil service, for patronage was their daily bread.

During the decade after his return Adams addressed nearly all these issues as a free-lance journalist, as a participant in the Liberal Republican movement, and as editor of the *North American Review*. While a reform professor at Harvard, he also sought to give intelligent direction to the American people. He was not alone in his concerns or in his reform tactics but belonged to a group of critics whom contemporaries (and historians) labeled *mugwumps*. The appellation meant "great leader" in American Indian, and it was given to them by their opponents, who believed they were effete and insincere. Although technically associated with the presidential election of 1884, the attitudes and tactics of the mugwumps were present in the late 1860s, and Adams generally shared them.

The typical mugwump was well-educated and of upper-middle- or upper-class background. Many were editors, a few were politicians, and most of the rest came from the ministry, academia, or the liberal professions of medicine and law, with a sprinkling of altruistic businessmen. Proper Bostonians and their counterparts in other cities tended to share the mugwump point of view. Mugwumps asserted that the country lacked the guidance of moral and intelligent leaders, and they resented the fact that postwar Americans had little use for their services in government. They concluded that the nation was in decline, losing sight of the founders' ideals. Political machines and ignorant immigrants, they lamented, had thoroughly corrupted the political system, as had greedy *nouveaux riches* businessmen.

For a time mugwumps hoped to use the Republican party as a vehicle for reform. The party originally had attracted antislavery idealists as well as most educated northerners. In the aftermath of the Civil War, however, it had degenerated and had become as corrupt as the Democratic organization. Refusing to place loyalty above conscience, mugwumps often supported whichever party best represented their views at a given time. When neither came close, they voted as independents or tried to form a third party.

A moralistic and independent political stance was nothing new to the Adamses, and Henry easily fell in with the mugwumps. John Stuart Mill's advice also made him a mugwump in politics and in his approach to reform. Indeed, Adams's first contact with the movement came when he decided to become a free-lance journalist, for there was a growing trend among newspapers and periodicals to disassociate from political parties. Before the war virtually all had been partisan. Now many appealed to a wider audience and reported the news more accurately by discarding party allegiances. They continued to endorse candidates but professed to do so solely on merit. Adams went one step further than most independent journalists, refusing to associate with any particular publication. He preferred to work on his own and to send articles to various newspapers and reviews, a luxury he could afford since his share of family investments brought him about $4,000 a year.

After spending several months with his parents at Quincy, Adams decided to settle at the focus of power and left for Washington. En route he stopped in New York armed with a letter of introduction to Edwin L. Godkin of the independent weekly *Nation,* for which he agreed to write occasional pieces. While there he ran into William Evarts, President Johnson's attorney general. Evarts belonged to an old and distinguished Boston family but had moved to New York. Adams and Evarts traveled together to the capital, and the attorney general asked his young companion to lodge with him until permanent accommodations could be found. Soon after they reached town, Evarts took Adams to meet President Johnson at the White House. The aspiring free-lancer also had an early reunion with William H. Seward, now secretary of state. Through Seward and Evarts he made the acquaintances of Treasury Secretary Hugh McCulloch and War Secretary John McAllister Schofield. He also began to meet reformers of the mugwump stripe. Missouri Senator Carl Schurz, a German refugee and hero of the Revolution of 1848, had championed reform causes since his arrival in the United States and would continue to do so until his death. David A. Wells, a fellow New Englander and graduate of Harvard's Lawrence Scientific School, was special commissioner of revenue. Wells's friend Jacob D. Cox was at the Interior Department. Several reform newspapermen rounded out the slate of new friends: young Samuel Bowles of the *Springfield* (Massachusetts) *Republican;* Murat Halstead of the *Cincinnati Commerical;* Henry Watterson of the Louisville *Courier-Journal.*

Adams was happy with his friends and was elated about Washington; the city charmed him as much as when he had first visited it as a child of twelve. The initial euphoria, however, did not save him from another attack of depres-

sion and self-doubt. In January he wrote to his brother
Charles that he was working hard on several articles yet felt
it was effort "absolutely thrown away." At the end of March
he told his confidant Charles Milnes Gaskell that long walks
had cured him of a recent "despondent fit," but added that
he was very thin and extremely bald. (Perhaps to compensate for his baldness, he had grown a beard.) Three weeks
later he complained to Gaskell of a liver ailment, which
the long walks also had alleviated. In June he lamented
that his "opinions and dislike for things in general" would
probably ruin his career. Meanwhile he continued to growl
at brother Charles, who was busy practicing law and writing
for the periodical press. As in the past his brother prescribed
aggressive activity, perhaps even a political life. Henry did
not like the advice, refusing, as he put it, to "go down
into the rough-and-tumble." It is possible that, to Henry,
Charles's blandishments sounded like the voices of three
generations of Adamses admonishing him not to sidestep
the duties imposed by his age, and that may be why he
ignored the advice. Whatever the reason, he became more
aware than ever of their differing personalities, and he despaired of trying to be like his older brother. "You like
roughness and strength; I like taste and dexterity. For God's
sake, let us go our ways and not try to be like each other."

In advising Henry, Charles no doubt had in mind his own
plans to make a career with the railroads, plans that led
eventually to the presidency of the Union Pacific. He must
have thought, too, of their older brother John, who had
abandoned the Republican party and had run for the gov-
ernorship of Massachusetts on the Democratic ticket. John
lost and would lose several more times, but his defeats never
deterred him from taking an active part in the affairs of his
day. Henry dismissed his brothers' examples because he
knew he lacked the proper temperament and because of his
old fears of criticism and failure. In journalism he could
continue where he already had proven himself. And if

Americans did not agree with his opinions, that was their fault, not his.

Yet Henry was soon lashing out at a multitude of problems and abuses. He submerged his fears and resentments in an ambitious campaign to inform fellow citizens, beginning with an assault on currency and taxation. He objected to the federal government's decision to finance the war through legal tender notes, or greenbacks. In "The Legal-Tender Act" (*Nation,* December 17, 1868) and then in "American Finance, 1865–1869" (*Edinburgh Review,* April 1869), he criticized such fiat money for producing financial instability. Since the Treasury did not redeem the greenbacks in either silver or gold, they fluctuated in value, thus discouraging sound investments while inviting speculation. Greenbacks were also dishonest in that debtors could pay off obligations with inflated currency. Most objectionable was the government's unwarranted authority to issue them. Declaring worthless pieces of paper to be money was not only unconstitutional, it violated laissez-faire principles in the marketplace. Adams still clung to the teachings of Mill as well as to the admonitions of old Professor Bowen: Government interference in the economy was both futile and dangerous.

Adams's approach to the tariff likewise rested in liberal economics. Protection disrupted the free flow of trade and was commonly the result of special interest lobbying, yielding larger profits for producers and higher prices for consumers. In addition, high tariffs were an incitement to corruption: The greater the duties, the greater was the temptation to bribe custom officials.

When it came to southern reconstruction, morality and laissez-faire continued to guide Adams. He treated the subject piecemeal in several articles, demanding that Washington leave the South alone to work out its own destiny. The task of restoration would be best accomplished by turning it over to the moral, intelligent, educated southern gentleman, who, it was hoped, would pursue a benign if paternalistic policy toward the helpless Negro. Like most northerners of the time, Adams did not believe that blacks were capable of self-rule after centuries of bondage; they had to trust the whites to uplift them slowly.

Turning to politics, Adams found the new Grant administration one of unparalleled corruption. Month after month scandal and wrongdoing sent Adams into fits of indignation. Two separate articles, each entitled "The Session" (*North American Review*, April 1869 and July 1870), blamed much of the public dishonesty on a breakdown in the balance of power in federal government. Central to the imbalance lay the spoils system. Under Andrew Jackson, himself a strong leader, the system had not undermined the presidency, but under less forceful successors, it had proven disastrous. Congressmen and senators, as a price for supporting a presidential candidate, demanded control of federal patronage within their districts or states, and weak chief executives were unable to resist them, patronage falling more and more under the legislative branch. The transfer accelerated in the immediate postwar period. Congress, controlled by Radical Republicans, passed the Tenure of Office Act, forbidding the president to remove appointees without senatorial consent. When Andrew Johnson violated the act and fired Secretary of War Stanton, the House impeached the president.

Congress's control of federal patronage meant that presidents would have to appeal to public opinion to support their right to select honest and competent officials without legislative interference. Adams confessed that he and many reform-minded journalists had supposed Grant would do just that. The general was not a professional politician; he had learned military discipline and administration; he seemed both honest and obstinate. Grant disappointed them immediately, unable to resist the pleas for favors from veterans, partisan supporters, and Republican congressmen.

Adams also deplored the quality of Grant's cabinet. The only member who demonstrated both honesty and capability was Attorney General Ebenezer Hoar of Massachusetts. Adams learned that Secretary of Navy Robeson had accumulated several hundred thousand dollars in kickbacks from contractors and that Secretary of War Belknap had lined his pockets by selling franchises for Indian trading posts. The corruption involved the White House even more closely. Grant's private secretary Orville Babcock had connived with Treasury agents and whiskey distillers to cheat the government out of taxes on liquor, and Vice-President Schuyler Colfax had accepted bribes from the Credit Mobilier Company, a subsidiary of the Union Pacific Railroad. Finally, the New York gold conspiracy revealed to Adams the depths of Grant's incompetence. He learned the details from his friend James A. Garfield, who chaired a House investigation into the affair, and Adams took it upon himself to broadcast the facts to the public. Perhaps he could arouse moral indignation to the point at which the American people would repudiate Grant once and for all.

In his "New York Gold Conspiracy" (*Westminster Review*, October 1870) Adams exposed the affair with great relish, beginning with a libelous characterization of the two perpetrators, Jim Fisk and Jay Gould. Gould, he wrote, suggested "survival from the family of spiders." He was "dark, sallow, reticent, and stealthy, with a trace of Jewish origin," and lacked the slightest conception of moral principle. The portrait of Fisk was no more flattering: "Personally Fisk was coarse, noisy, boastful, ignorant, the type of a young butcher in appearance and mind." Adams went on to describe the two men's machinations to corner the New York gold market. Their plan was to buy gold with greenbacks, which private sellers would accept at a premium; that is, every $1 of gold might cost $1.30 in greenbacks. If Fisk and Gould bought enough gold, they could force its price to a much higher level and then unload, reaping a huge profit. The major obstacle was the United States Treasury, which could force down the price of the metal by dumping reserves on the New York market.

The two conspirators bribed Abel R. Corbin, the president's brother-in-law, to introduce them to Grant. Fisk and Gould wined and dined the president, trying to convince him that their scheme was entirely for the good of the economy. They only wanted to raise the price of gold so that farmers might receive higher prices at harvest time. Although Grant was somewhat suspicious, he did not contradict them and took no action to thwart their project. Believing they had neutralized the government, Fisk and Gould proceeded to force the greenback price of a gold dollar from $1.34 to $1.62. At this juncture one of the president's advisors convinced him that the financiers were engaged in disreputable activities, and Grant ordered Treasury Secretary Boutwell to sell bullion. Through Corbin, Gould received advance word of the order and was able to sell his gold in time to avoid disaster. He failed to pass the word along to Fisk, however, who was ruined. Hurt, too, were thousands of brokers, bankers, and businessmen who had had to buy gold at inflated prices in order to meet legitimate obligations. Fisk and Gould escaped legal action, for they had broken no existing laws.

In his article Adams explained how the two had acquired the funds with which to make their enormous purchases of gold. Having controlling interests in the Erie Railroad as well as in a large New York bank, they had used the resources of both to finance their venture. The adventurers had wielded great concentrations of capital in order to amass personal fortunes and in so doing had injured many innocent people and challenged the sovereignty of the United States government itself. Adams was struck at once by the potential danger of modern capitalism. "For the first time since the creation of these enormous corporate bodies," he charged, "one of them has shown its power for mischief, and has proved itself able to override and trample on law, custom, decency, and every restraint known to society." He hoped that exposure would outrage the public and that the force of opinion alone might civilize big business; to ask for government regulation of the corporations would violate laissez-faire.

Nonetheless, Adams realized that a general appeal to public opinion might not be sufficient and that people of his persuasion had to gain the ear of government. He therefore proposed, in an article entitled "Men and Things in Washington" (*Nation,* November 25, 1869), that Washington needed a gentlemen's club on the English model, where legislators, diplomats, administrators, and enlightened citizens could exchange views. Without such a club government officials might hear only the views of the spoilmen, party hacks, and special interest lobbies. The suggestion was a testament both to Adams's admiration of English institutions and to his naiveté about American politics. The government of Great Britain remained largely in the hands of the landed gentry and the educated upper middle class. With a much wider distribution of political power in the United States, determination of public policy in exclusive clubs was unacceptable.

By the spring of 1870, having exerted so much effort on journalistic polemics, Adams longed to escape Washington and the grind of one article after another. Accordingly, he decided to spend the summer in Europe. He was certain that the American experiment was in trouble. Citizens did not have the good sense to elect the most honest and capable candidates. Government was helpless to cope with reconstruction, civil service, the currency, and the tariff. He had done his best to lead the way; time would tell if he and his cohorts were making any headway.

Intent on enjoying himself abroad, he set sail for England and reached Liverpool the first week of June. After several weeks visiting Gaskell and other friends, he left for the Continent, where he received a letter from Harvard President Charles William Eliot offering him an assistant professorship in history. Eliot, who had become Harvard's new head the year before, wanted bright, energetic young men to help overhaul the institution. Adams politely declined; he preferred to continue in journalism for another ten or fifteen years, after which he might consider such an appointment.

Adams returned to America in September to find that Eliot had not taken his refusal seriously. Indeed, he had discussed the professorship with Charles Francis Adams, who agreed that Henry should accept. Henry was also offered direction of the *North American Review,* editor Ephraim Gurney having been made dean of the Harvard faculty. The elder Adams thought Henry should accept the second post as well, since the two positions would allow him to settle into something more permanent and respectable than freelance writing. His brothers seconded the recommendation and Henry finally conceded. He would receive $2,000 a year for the teaching and nothing for his work at the *Review,* but with his income from the family, it was enough for a comfortable living.

The return to the Boston area was a mistake. By moving to Washington Adams had cut loose from the family and New England and had established something of a separate identity. Now he was returning to the scenes and associations of childhood and youth, and in a few years he would regret the move. Initially, however, the change was agreeable because the editorship permitted him to keep a hand in reform journalism. By contributing pieces himself and soliciting from friends, he could turn the *Review* into a reform vehicle. He also looked forward to joining Eliot's campaign to remodel the college, thinking of it as one more attack upon the inadequacies of the age.

No sooner had Adams occupied his posts at Cambridge than he found much else to occupy his mind. He met and fell in love with Marian Hooper. Clover, as all her friends and relatives called her, came from one of New England's first families. Her father Robert Hooper could trace his lineage back to seventeenth-century Massachusetts, and he had added greatly to a modest inheritance through shrewd investments. Clover's mother Ellen Sturgis was the daughter of Captain William Sturgis, who, like the Brookses, had amassed wealth in maritime trade. The Sturgises, too, traced their forebears back to seventeenth-century New England. Henry and Marian were wed in June 1872, and after an extended honeymoon abroad, occupied a house in Boston's fashionable Back Bay. Henry had made an exemplary match and settled down to the life of a proper Boston gentleman.

Professionally, his first task was to come to grips with the classroom, for his editorial duties did not begin until January 1871. In light of Adams's dearth of special training in history, a professorship might make little sense. But only a handful of Americans were professional historians, the subject being primarily an adjunct to literature or philosophy. For some time, however, the German universities had treated history as a separate discipline and applied to it the rules of scientific research, an approach that Eliot wanted Adams to follow at Harvard. He believed that his assistant professor was intelligent and energetic enough to learn and to use the German methods.

Eliot's inaugural address had vowed to turn Harvard into a great world university, an aspiration shared by Yale, Princeton, and the new Johns Hopkins. Eliot wished to introduce more scientific courses, to give students a wide choice among subjects, and to make Harvard men into creative, independent individuals who could provide the talent, the intelligence, and the leadership that the country needed to solve its complex modern problems. On these points Adams and he heartily agreed. Both desired to see an aristocracy of talent and virtue in control of the nation's institutions, public as well as private.

Adams was an instant success in the classroom. His initial assignment was to teach medieval history, a course limited only by the dates A.D. 800–1649. Several years later he instituted the first full-fledged American history classes at Harvard and also the college's first graduate seminar. In the beginning he barely stayed a day ahead of his students, but this did not detract in the slightest from his performance; he was a born teacher. Students recalled that he treated them with dignity and respect rather than as underlings. They also remembered that he interlarded his lectures with wit and satire and regarded nothing as sacred, encouraging them to have a critical attitude toward every authority and source. He was more interested in giving them a reflective approach to the past than he was in filling their heads with random facts. In addition, he tried to make them see that the present was a product of historical forces, for they could not tackle contemporary difficulties unless they understood their antecedents.

Adams stated his ideas on educational reform in an article for the January 1872 *North American Review*. "Harvard College 1786–87" was ostensibly a review of two recently published accounts of student life in the eighteenth century. Adams, however, took the liberty of making extensive comments on the need for change. Both accounts, but especially the one covering the academic year 1786–87, argued that faculty and administration too often had been more interested in their own welfare than in their students. They viewed the college as a vested interest, as a means of professional advancement or of making a living. The students' accounts also suggested that teachers and college officials placed insurmountable barriers between themselves and the students. If such memoirs taught anything, Adams reflected, they showed that "no system of education can be very successful which does not have the scholar as its chief object of interest; a principle which may sound like a truism, but which, in fact, will be found to have rarely been put into practice on any great scale." He tried hard to follow his own advice.

All the while Adams remained interested in politics. He turned to several Washington associates for articles in his first issue of the *Review,* asking Carl Schurz, David A. Wells, and Jacob D. Cox to submit pieces. Only Schurz came through with a work on his reform principles, but brother Charles saved the day with his "Government and the Railroads."

Charles's article was one in a series he had written to expose railroad fraud and mismanagement. In September the brothers brought out a collection of their periodical writings under the title *Chapters of Erie and Other Essays.* It included Henry's "Legal-Tender Act" and "New York Gold Conspiracy," along with Charles's "An Erie Raid" and "A Chapter of Erie." Sympathetic reviewers in the United States and Britain had high praise for the book.

Meanwhile Adams and other mugwumps began to discuss the 1872 presidential election. By then they were completely disgusted with Grant and the Republican party to which most of the reformers belonged. Yet they were not ready to abandon the party altogether, believing that it promised the best chance for reform. Republicans had opposed slavery and had presided over its liquidation. During the war the party had given the country its first national currency since the demise of the Second Bank of the United States, and it had created the land grant colleges. After the war Republicans had tried to take a comprehensive approach to reconstruction. Later they would sponsor civil service reform, the Interstate Commerce Act, and the Sherman Antitrust Act. Although the legislation was too little too late, all were attempts to deal with pressing national problems. Whether or not mugwumps subscribed to each of these initiatives was unimportant; that the Republican party was amenable to action and change gave encouragement.

The Democrats had little chance of becoming a reform party. They could not discipline their ranks on the national level, being, as they were, a combination of conservative southerners and provincial northern organizations. In addition, the party had enlisted many recent immigrants who did not share the attitudes of men like Henry Adams. Irish Catholics, for instance, often rejected the possibility of reform on this earth, and the Irish urban machines despised even the hint of civil service legislation and an end to the spoils system.

Thus the mugwumps were drawn to the Republican party, although they were distraught over its performance in recent years. It had descended to the worst patronage politics, and the Grant scandals were unparalleled in history. Convinced that the party needed a moral housecleaning, the reformers swore to deny Grant a second term and to restore their party to its original high ideals. As early as November 1870 Adams had attended a meeting in New York City that had adopted resolutions in support of revenue and civil service reform and had sharply criticized the Grant presidency. A consolidation of this group and similar ones throughout the country, having concluded that it was impossible to work through regular channels, founded the Liberal Republican party. (Their choice of the word *liberal* stemmed from adherence to laissez-faire ideas.) Regarding themselves as true Republicans, the reformers were determined to keep the old label and hoped to convert the whole party.

Many reformers whom Adams had met in Washington belonged to the new party: Wells, Cox, Bowles, Godkin, Watterson, Halstead, and Schurz, Schurz becoming the organizational force behind the party. Also joining were Charles Francis Adams, Jr., William Cullen Bryant of the *New York Evening Post,* and Arthur George Sedgwick of the *Atlantic Monthly*. The reform party supported lower tariffs, southern home rule, and civil service and currency reform.

The genteel reformers organized a Liberal Republican convention, which met in Cincinnati in May 1872. Adams refused to attend, suspecting that political maneuvering would dominate the convention, and events proved him right. Many Liberals wanted to nominate Charles Francis Adams, Sr., as their presidential candidate, a man of impeccable morality and high ideals. The elder Adams, always hesitant to align with any group that might compromise his freedom of judgment and action, said only that he would consider a draft, although Henry and Charles, Jr., tried to elicit a statement in favor of Liberal principles. The remainder of the Liberals were divided in their opinions. The convention had brought together many groups of varying persuasions, united only by their hostility to Grant. Some cared exclusively for free trade; others saw civil service reform as the most pressing problem; and several vied for the nomination only to advance their own careers. In the end the conventioneers had to compromise, and they selected Horace Greeley, editor of the New York *Tribune*. The original and more idealistic elements of the party were furious, defeated by the very tactics they opposed.

It was some consolation that Greeley was honest and had upheld various reform schemes, though several were bizarre. The only segment of the Liberals that he alienated totally were the staunch free traders, for he was an outspoken protectionist. The Democrats, desperate to win the presidency after being out of power since Buchanan, overlooked Greeley's reform principles and also nominated him. In November, however, Grant defeated him in a landslide, Greeley carrying only seven states, all in the South. Without Democratic backing he would have lost even these.

Greeley's defeat showed that the vast majority of voters did not share the Liberals' disgust with President Grant. For most northerners the war hero represented the American dream come true: a man who had risen from humble origins to the highest office in the land.

Nor did the electorate accept the Liberals' reform principles. The reformers could not understand that for millions of recent immigrants the so-called spoils system was their only opportunity for rapid advancement. Those who met discrimination when trying to enter skilled trades or who could not afford much education made their votes work for them. They supported political machines, which then offered the reward of a job on the public payroll. Adams and his well-to-do associates further failed to recognize the justifiable fears of a professional bureaucracy. Once entrenched, career civil servants often looked upon their positions as personal property and lost touch with citizens and their concerns. Only frequent rotation in office, as Jackson had maintained, would check the abuse.

On protection, at least, Greeley agreed with the general public. Championing free trade would have made Greeley's defeat worse, again proving the unpopularity of the reformers' views. The issue of protection, in fact, was about the only one around which voters from many walks of life could rally. In the following three decades Republicans won the presidency time after time, in part by assuring farmers, laborers, and businessmen that high tariffs brought prosperity to all. This issue, as much as any other, enabled the party to forge a centralized organization by 1896. At last Republican presidents could make their weight felt in Congress and guard the rights of the executive branch. Adams and the Liberals failed to appreciate this success and abandoned the party, one more instance of their impracticality.

The Liberals' laissez-faire reconstruction policies had an equally dim chance of winning at the polls. Too many northerners still wanted to reshape the South in their own image. But when the federal government finally did restore home rule, it left blacks to the mercy of local inhabitants.

Adams and the reformers had a good case in the currency question, but their demand for a return to the gold standard was insufficient. The limited supply of gold did not increase at the same rate as the production of goods and services, nor did it decrease in times of depression. The result was periodic inflation and deflation. Not until the twentieth century would the American economy enjoy a truly flexible currency, and then only after it had abandoned a domestic gold standard and the government had assumed control of the money supply.

But of all the Liberals' unpopular stands, it was the refusal to play politics that led to their downfall in 1872. They had no chance of wresting control from professional politicians who understood that compromise and distribution of jobs and favors were the only routes open to winning elections and passing legislation. Adams was more unrealistic in this regard than some others, for he refused even to take part in the party's convention. He could not grasp, as did patricians like Henry Cabot Lodge and Theodore Roosevelt, that the best chance for reform was through the system.

Inadequate though his politics were, Adams did not give up. He continued to solicit and to welcome reform writings in the *North American Review*. Most of the time he was too busy to contribute full articles himself and limited his offerings to book reviews. As the centennial year neared, he decided to devote the entire January 1876 issue to analyzing the evolution of American thought during its first century of national existence. The issue would try to ascertain whether the American experiment had indeed produced a higher intellectual development. As Adams explained to astronomer Simon Newcomb, he wished to know "whether and to what degree Americans should feel satisfaction or disappointment at the result of a century's [intellectual] activity." He asked six men, each an authority in his field, to assess the movement in his discipline over the past one hundred years. The subjects for consideration were science, economics, politics, education, religion, and law.

Adams's contributors by and large echoed his belief that

the country needed more and stronger intellectual leadership if the American experiment were to succeed. Newcomb,
head of the U.S. Naval Observatory, admitted in his piece
that Americans deserved high praise for their practical ap-
plications of science, but he faulted them for not compre-
hending the importance of abstract research as a forerunner
to practical solutions. In a country where all questions, economic, political, and social, were becoming more complex
and sophisticated, the need for a sounder abstract framework was more pressing than ever. Unless Americans rose
above mere tinkering with problems and tried to fathom
the natural laws behind them, there was slight chance for
intelligent, lasting solutions.

Charles F. Dunbar, professor of economics at Harvard,
reiterated Newcomb's advice. Ironically, the country that
achieved such astounding wealth so quickly had contributed
almost nothing to economic thought. He joined Newcomb
in blaming America's practical bent, which he attributed
to the necessity of conquering a wilderness. The time had
come, however, to take a more comprehensive and theoreti-
cal approach to economic events. In the past rapid material
growth had tended to obscure blunders in policy, but as the
economy matured, ignorant decisions would lead to disaster.
Perhaps then politicians and public would demand more informed economic policy. Short of this eventuality, better
economic education and the efforts of opinion molders
might alert the nation before it was too late.

William Graham Sumner, professor of political and social
sciences at Yale, also lamented the paucity of intelligent
leadership. Very early in the Republic honest, educated
men had abandoned politics, finding greater satisfactions
in other areas. They had done so largely because the common voter, increasingly imbued with democratic sentiments,
spurned persons of propriety and learning. Yet Sumner did
not despair. An unparalleled constitutional system might

still work as the founders had intended. Sumner hoped that the concerns of vocal reformers would become widespread enough to save the system.

Daniel Coit Gilman, president of Johns Hopkins University, underlined the importance of education in a democratic society. Unfortunately, American instruction was wanting on all three levels — primary, secondary, and university. Elementary schools, open to anyone who wanted to attend, had generated wide literacy, but they as well as secondary schools and colleges typically relied on rote learning and did not inculcate the analytical manner of thinking that was needed to cope with the intricacies of modern life. He hoped that the changes at Johns Hopkins and elsewhere would help remedy these inadequacies.

J. Lewis Diman, former clergyman and professor of history and economics at Brown, contributed the article on theology, and G. T. Bispham, Philadelphia attorney and mugwump, authored the piece on law. Both found faults with American accomplishments, but generally they were more encouraging than the other four contributors. Diman decried the lack of original contributions in theology, yet he was encouraged by the spread of religious sentiment in the United States since 1776, there being far more churches per capita in the centennial year than a hundred years before. The churches had placed great emphasis on the practice of Christianity in daily life and had raised the country's moral bearing. Bispham applauded the Republic for its achievement in constitution writing and in the codification of law. The nation's laws also had become more humane than Europe's and merited praise for their intelligence, practicality, and morality.

Although the American people succeeded in practical solutions, they had disappointed the intellectual hopes of the early Republic. Adams shared the mixed conclusions of his authors, particularly in his review of Hermann von Holst's *Constitutional and Political History of the United States*

(*North American Review,* October 1876). The greatest weakness of the Constitution, von Holst had proclaimed, was its concessions to states' rights. Adams countered that such concessions, while objectionable in theory, were a practical necessity given the realities of state autonomy in 1787. Practice had in fact permitted the Constitution to work in favor of national unity. The document had given the central government much potential, and officials had invoked it whenever circumstances permitted. Now that secession had been smashed, Adams believed that federal power was freer than ever to deal with increasingly national problems. Americans, he concluded, were "quite right in believing that, above all the details of human weakness and corruption, there will appear in more and more symmetry the real majesty and force of the national movement." If his compatriots could admit the need for intelligent and talented leadership, the Constitution would provide the framework enabling them to outstrip the Old World in almost every respect.

In the meantime Adams was concerned over the 1876 presidential campaign. The Liberal Republican movement had collapsed, but its leaders still held their mugwump convictions. Calling themselves independent liberals, they proposed to exert their weight by supporting whichever party nominated a reform candidate. Adams drafted a form letter inviting independents to gather immediately after the Republican convention to decide if they could accept the candidate. At the same time he embarked on a scheme to buy the *Boston Post* as a mouthpiece for independent opinions, offering to take $5,000 in stock.

Summer came and all Adams's plans went awry. The *Post* project fell through, as did the meeting of independents. Schurz agreed to support the Republican ticket in exchange for a position in the cabinet, thus yielding to political corruption as far as Adams was concerned. Nor was he happy with either of the candidates, Republican Rutherford B.

Hayes or Democrat Samuel J. Tilden. In "Independents in the Canvass" (*North American Review*, October 1876) he and brother Charles elaborated the dissatisfaction. They asked independents to ignore all the "rubbish" of the campaign: what the contenders did or did not do during the war, "the charges and countercharges made as to their transactions in mules, their stealing railroads, plundering widows and orphans, . . . the number of watches they own, and the date at which they may have purchased pianos." They also should not heed official party platforms, since both parties were taking evasive stands on the issues.

Of the important questions in the campaign, the Adamses singled out civil service reform, upon which all else hinged. A victory for Hayes was not likely to bring the desired result, for a Republican Congress would not give up its control of patronage to the president. If Tilden won, on the other hand, the office-starved Democrats certainly would not insist on nonpartisan, merit appointments. Nevertheless, the authors urged independents to vote Democratic. Tilden at least might refuse the patronage demands of a Republican Congress. And wholesale firings of civil servants would so outrage public opinion as to ensure reform in 1880. Once more the Adamses put their faith in moral anger instead of direct political action, continuing to believe that reform had no chance until the public was shaken from its apathy. "Unless the evil is checked," the brothers warned, "our political system must break down and some new experiment must be substituted in its place." Clearly, neither had learned anything about practical politics.

The brothers' contribution was not the only reform article in the October issue of the *Review*. In his editorial capacity Adams had enlisted several other authors for the *Review*'s own canvass. There were articles on the "Whiskey Ring" and the "Tweed Ring" along with a blast against continuing federal interference in the South. The pieces were so vituperative in their criticism of American politics, and particularly of the Republican record under Grant, that the *Review*'s publishers feared financial repercussions and disavowed all responsibility. The issue was a sellout, and the *Review* went through a second printing for the first time in its history. Adams was quite proud, but he used the publishers' initial irritation as a pretext for resigning the editorship. Actually he had tired of his duties and resented the time spent on them. Soon thereafter he quit his professorship as well. More than most he was bored with an activity once he had mastered it. Before him was an endless succession of students, classrooms, and seminars, one blending into the other. In September 1876 he had written Gaskell, "I am just beginning my grind at the university wheel."

By the time Adams decided to leave his two posts, he had been working for nearly a decade to save the American people from their errors. He had believed that exposing corruption and ignorance and offering the public better candidates were enough. Although he was not ready in 1876 to turn his back on the national experiment, he was depressed at the lack of reform. Besides, he had become much interested in writing history, proposing that he had to delve deeper into the American past in order to understand present dilemmas.

History of the Experiment: Part I

ADAMS'S DECISION to leave Harvard and the *North American Review* was brought about as much by his old dissatisfaction with certain aspects of Boston society as by his boredom with teaching and editing. He complained to his former graduate student Henry Cabot Lodge that the city grew more provincial every day. To his old friend Charles Milnes Gaskell he wrote in the same vein: "Boston is a curious place. Its business in life is to breed and to educate. The parent lives for his children; the child, when educated himself, becomes a parent, or becomes an educator, or is both. But no further result is ever reached." There was "no society worth the name, no wit, no intellectual energy or competition, no clash of minds or of schools."

Adams exaggerated. The area had more than its share of writers and thinkers, including James Russell Lowell, William Dean Howells, William James, and Oliver Wendell Holmes, but Adams did not savor their company. And nearing his fortieth birthday, he had begun to fear that staying at Harvard would lock him into a routine that might prove impossible to escape. At the commencement of middle age, life was passing him by all too quickly. A professorship, six years heading the *Review*, and scores of articles certainly were respectable. However, all the successful Adamses had written and published, pursuits that were only ancillary to greater distinctions. Remaining in the city of his birth reinforced his feelings of inadequacy, for all around him were reminders of his forebears' triumphs. He knew then that the move back to Boston had been a mistake.

Another factor motivating Adams to leave Boston was his growing desire to write serious history, which was frustrated by his heavy duties at Harvard. The wish to concentrate on historical writing overtook him as he read, reflected, and taught. By 1876 he was convinced that a careful examination of the American past was instrumental in apprehending present difficulties. A decade as reform journalist and editor had achieved little so far as he could tell. His desire to write history also sprang from the hope of literary applause, like that of George Bancroft and Francis Parkman. Success would give him the further satisfaction of a career all his own.

During the next decade and a half Adams produced an impressive amount of historical writing. He turned out biographies of Albert Gallatin and John Randolph and edited three volumes of Gallatin's papers. He also completed a nine-volume history of the United States covering the years 1801–1817. In the midst of these projects, and partly as a diversion from them, he wrote two novels, *Democracy* and *Esther*.

This time of steady scholarship and writing was the happiest in Adams's life. No small part of his mood was due to the return to Washington, a move dictated by his old love for the city and his continuing fascination with politics. In a letter to Gaskell he tried to convey his delight in the new home: "We have made a great leap in the world. . . . The fact is I gravitate to a capital by a primary law of nature. This is the only place in America where society amuses me, or where life offers variety." He was filled with hope for himself and his wife and extolled to his English friend the beauties of the federal district. He added that he was optimistic about the nation's future: "I belong to the class of people who have great faith in this country and who believe that in another century it will be saying . . . the last word of civilization."

Henry and Marian Adams easily found a place in Washington society, even though they wielded no political power and had not long resided in the capital. Both were from old and wealthy New England families, and in addition, Adams descended from two presidents; these advantages gained them immediate entry everywhere. Indeed, it was not long until they were social arbiters of sorts.

They rented a spacious and fashionable house on Lafayette Square at 1501 H Street and filled it with the decorative objects of the day, with porcelains, bronzes, tapestries, paintings, and bric-a-brac, much of it collected during their travels abroad. A combined income of $25,000 a year allowed them to entertain in style, and within several months an invitation from the Adamses was highly coveted. They eventually established in their home something akin to the European salon. Henry's years in England and on the Continent had taught him how influential the salon might be as an informal assemblage of politicians, writers, artists, critics, musicians, and socialites. Meeting on a regular basis, its members discussed a variety of topics, varying in emphasis according to the group's composition and interests. In such a setting the bright, creative individual might obtain the ear of politicians and thus have an impact upon councils of state. Had Adams been born in England or France, he would have found little difficulty moving between the worlds of politics and writing. Such an opportunity was not available in the United States, but he and Marian tried their best to establish an atmosphere where the better and more capable elements of the city mingled on an informal basis with enlightened public officials. In doing so they partly fulfilled Adams's earlier plans for an elite club in the capital.

Nearly every afternoon a dozen or more select personalities assembled at the Adams tea table. Many evenings, when not attending functions away from home, the hosts asked six or eight to dinner. Spending his days probing the politics of the early republic, Henry passed his late afternoons and evenings with policymakers of his own generation. He thereby kept abreast of the American experiment as it manifested itself in government.

The Adamses' guests might find themselves chatting with Carl Schurz, now secretary of interior and apparently forgiven for his apostasy from independent ranks. Or they might strike up a conversation with Secretary of State Evarts and Congressman Abram Hewitt, both dedicated reformers. Several associates from free-lance days were likely to be there, particularly Jacob D. Cox and David A. Wells. Also commonly present were Senator and Mrs. Donald Cameron, two of the Adamses' newer friends. Although boss of Pennsylvania's corrupt Republican machine, the senator was acceptable largely because of his beautiful and lively wife Elizabeth, the niece of General William T. Sherman and Senator John Sherman. Similarly of recent acquaintance was Senator Lucius Q. C. Lamar, ex-Confederate army officer and diplomat and lately a spokesman for reconciliation between North and South. Other and more colorful new associates were General Edward Beale, wilderness explorer and Mexican War hero, and Aristarchi Bey, the eccentric and cynical Turkish minister.

A variety of out-of-town guests constantly dropped in: Marian's father and brother, members of Henry's family, E. L. Godkin of the *Nation*, Henry James on one of his infrequent visits to the United States, and sculptor Augustus Saint-Gaudens. But especially welcome were Clarence King and John Hay. Adams first met Hay during the secession winter of 1860–1861. Born the same year as Adams, he had come to Washington as private secretary to Abraham Lincoln. Hay had led a rich and strenuous life after Lincoln's assassination. He had been secretary to the legations at Paris, Vienna, and Madrid, had written for the New York *Tribune,* had helped run his father-in-law's business, and presently was assistant secretary of state. Complementing these accomplishments were a volume of poetry and a travel book about Spain; ahead lay his ten-volume biography of Lincoln with John Nicolay, his novel *Breadwinners,* and his brilliant achievements as ambassador to Great Britain and secretary of state. Adams found Hay constantly amusing, full of stories about Lincoln or his boyhood in rural Illinois.

Equally cherished was Clarence King, born, as were Hay and Adams, in 1838. Adams met him while on a trip to the Rockies in the summer of 1871. Almost single-handedly King had persuaded Congress to authorize the massive Fortieth Parallel Survey, a geographical survey of the region between Colorado and California, and later he was a moving force in creating the permanent U.S. Geological Survey, which he headed from 1878 to 1881. His reports of the Survey's findings were classics of precise yet engaging scientific prose, and his *Mountaineering in the Sierra Nevada,* half tall tale and half fact, thrilled thousands.

Much of King's and Hay's attraction for Adams lay in their active lives and want of New England credentials. While gentlemen of accomplishment, they were leagues apart from austere, proper Bostonians and complemented Adams's retiring personality. King and Hay and his wife Clara always felt at home with the Adamses, fondly referring to themselves as the "Five of Hearts."

These close friendships demonstrated that Henry and Marian Adams were not always snobs. The descendant of a midwestern farmer or manufacturer might be as welcome as a Boston blue blood so long as he or she had talent, charm, or intelligence and so long as the Adamses took a fancy to the person. They even overlooked the shortcomings of one spouse in order to enjoy the company of the other, Donald Cameron and his machine politics being a prime example. For the most part, however, corruptionists were shunned, the *bête noire* of the Adamses' circle being Senator James G. Blaine, who had supposedly taken bribes from the railroads. Henry and Marian refused to invite the Blaines to their home and scrupulously avoided all social engagements where they were present, continuing the practice even after Garfield made Blaine secretary of state. In one of her weekly letters to her father, Marian wrote that Blaine "represents the corruption element as thoroughly as any man can." It was their duty to punish dishonest politicians in every possible way, including social ostracism.

The Adamses' social life helped Henry professionally, for it opened doors to historical research. Secretary of State Evarts gave him access to diplomatic papers, providing him with his own desk in the department's library. During their first years in Washington Adams spent about five hours daily researching and writing history. His approach to both derived from his teaching at Harvard, his admiration of the German historical school, and his reading of nineteenth-century historians and philosophers of history. From teaching he retained the idea that the past was a key to the present, and the Germans gave him models of how to treat history scientifically. This orientation was reinforced in the writings of Auguste Comte, Herbert Spencer, Henry Buckle, and Hippolyte Taine.

In Spencer and Comte Henry found strong agreement with his assertion that the present had grown out of the past. Spencer compared society to a living organism. Like the biological evolutionists, he proposed that society progressed from a simpler to a more complex state. Although Adams did not accept all Spencer's points, he found Spencer's emphasis upon the continuity and growth of history intriguing. Comte's development from religious to metaphysical to positive was similar to Spencer's scheme in that it, too, posited a social progression.

In Buckle and Taine Adams discovered more about how to reduce the incidents of history to larger themes and laws. According to Buckle any movement or epoch in history was the product of climate, food, soil, and the appearance of the physical environment. The harsh weather of northern Europe, Buckle believed, had resulted in a vigorous, industrious people. The milder weather of southern Europe, on the other hand, had produced a lethargic, unimaginative population. Taine traced historical development to such factors as race, milieu, and time. Race was the general character of a people and resulted from inherited as well as environmental factors. Milieu was the climate and geography, while time was the chronological element.

Having digested the works of these historians and philosophers, Adams embarked on his own writing. His first major historical works were the biographies of Albert Gallatin and John Randolph. Able to stand alone as separate studies, they became preliminaries to his great work, the *History of the United States of America during the Administrations of Thomas Jefferson and James Madison*. In the biographies he experimented with various types of historical writing and began to formulate theories about the early Republic.

The *Life of Albert Gallatin,* along with a three-volume edition of his writings, appeared in the summer of 1879, projects commissioned by Gallatin's last surviving son. Adams made no attempt to impose on his subject the elaborate framework called for by Buckle and Taine but did see Gallatin as the instrument of external forces over which he had little control. That Gallatin consistently did his best within narrow circumstances was evidence to Adams of his noble character. Gallatin emerged as the ideal statesman, a model even John Adams could have admired. Gallatin also personified democratic faith, a man determined to make the American experiment a shining success. His

failure to realize that dream and his eventual disillusionment made him an attractive subject and afforded Adams
ample opportunity to pass moral judgment on the inability
of fellow citizens to live up to the founders' hopes.

Born in Geneva, Switzerland, to an old, distinguished
family, Gallatin learned some of the same lessons as the
young Henry Adams. Gallatin believed that society had to
be grounded in wisdom and virtue if people were to experience happiness and prosperity, and that it was the duty of
talented individuals to serve others. But unlike the Adamses,
Gallatin was optimistic about the mass of humanity. In
spite of a stern Calvinist upbringing, he was an early ad-
mirer of Rousseau and was determined to settle in the
American wilderness where he could live a pristine life.
Accordingly, he staked a claim in the barely tamed reaches
of western Pennsylvania. Entering Pennsylvania politics as
a Jeffersonian Republican, Gallatin rose from one elective
office to another, securing a seat in the U.S. House of Representatives in 1794. By the end of the decade he was leader
of the Jeffersonians in Congress.

The real drama of Gallatin's life began when Jefferson,
victorious in the election of 1800, made him secretary of
treasury. According to Adams the Treasury was and continued to be the key to all domestic affairs. The volume of
taxation and expenditure was a sure indication of the scope
of government, and the nature of spending largely determined the outlines of domestic policy. Whoever controlled
the purse ran the public household. Gallatin thus played
a central role in Jefferson's resolve to make democracy
work.

Beneath the new president's plans lay a set of assump-
tions about human nature and politics that Gallatin shared.
They and their close associate James Madison wished to
initiate a scheme that "was broad as society itself, and aimed
at providing for and guiding the moral and material development of a new era, — a fresh race of men." The great

majority were basically moral and rational, and if left alone they would rule themselves in peace, prosperity, and happiness. Citizens had no need of powerful government, especially at the national level. What government they required was best exercised by state and local authorities over whom they could watch closely, thereby protecting their legitimate interests.

Federal tasks were accordingly simple and few: to protect the country from foreign invasion, to adjudicate disputes among the states, and to enforce a handful of criminal statutes. Above all, the central government was to keep to the letter of the Constitution and to refrain from expanding national power whenever possible. States' rights and strict adherence to the Constitution went hand in hand and were the bulwarks of the Jeffersonian philosophy. Among its most important manifestations were severely limited government and freedom from public debt. Americans should enjoy the fruits of their labor without the burden of interest payments on national obligations. Indeed, Jeffersonians looked with horror upon Alexander Hamilton's espousal of a permanent federal debt, which benefited the wealthy and encouraged deficit spending. Furthermore, license to borrow encouraged aggressive designs against other countries and was reminiscent of decadent English practices. If European rulers taxed their subjects into bankruptcy, interfered with their private rights, and plunged their nations into incessant and pointless wars, the United States would do just the opposite. Americans would show the rest of the world how to live in happiness, freedom, and peace. Jefferson and his followers viewed their people as "standing outside the political movement of Europe" and able to follow their own course.

For a time it looked as if the experiment was going to succeed. The administration and Congress cooperated to abolish internal taxes; they reduced the national debt annually; they practically disbanded the army and the navy.

Meanwhile foreign trade flourished and tariff revenues mounted; soon Jefferson and Gallatin were faced with the problem of how to spend Treasury surpluses. Then disaster struck. The wars that had raged intermittently in Europe since the French Revolution resumed, and American shipping again was the target of both British and French attacks. Armed retaliation would spell the death of Jefferson's system. Taxes would soar; the debt would increase alarmingly; Americans would throw themselves into the never-ending quarrels of decadent Europe. The president's alternative was an embargo on trade from the United States. But the embargo made it necessary for Gallatin, the officer most responsible for upholding the trade restrictions, to use force against his own people. He directed armed guards to patrol the wharves and revenue cutters to intercept smugglers, disasterously expensive measures at a time when tariff collections were declining. To many it seemed the United States had turned into a despot that forbade its citizens to dispose of their goods and property as they wished.

Gallatin, bitterly unhappy, did as the law directed. Under Jefferson's successor Madison his task was even more distasteful. The embargo and subsequent trade restrictions had not chastened the country's tormenters and had brought discord at home. Britain and France would respect armed force alone, and only war would unify the American people. Much as he hated the prospect, Gallatin tried to prepare the nation for battle. He urged the building of more ships; he advised Congress to construct fortifications and military roads and to stockpile arms and ammunition; and he supported the recharter of the Bank of the United States. When war broke out in 1812, he advocated higher taxes rather than massive deficit spending. Unfortunately his words of wisdom went unheeded; at every turn less capable men in the legislature dismissed his proposals. As a result, the country was woefully unprepared and had great difficulty financing the war without the professional services and stable currency of a national bank.

The War of 1812 was the final blow to Gallatin's dreams; forces beyond Jefferson's or Madison's control had dictated the result. Europe did not allow the United States to stand back from its bickerings but forced Americans to fight for the rights of a sovereign nation. In addition, the two presidents had overestimated their people's capacity for reason and self-restraint. Americans refused to obey the embargo and rallied only to a cry for revenge and the prospect of conquering British Canada. In the end Americans showed themselves to be as violent as any inhabitants of the Old World.

By the second year of the war Gallatin knew it was time to leave the Treasury. He had made too many enemies in Congress and was more of an impediment to the administration than a help. When Madison appointed him special emissary to Russia to negotiate peace through the czar's good offices, he gladly took the post. Recognizing that his calmness of mind and good judgment fitted him to be a diplomat, he made the best of circumstances and served the country as occasion permitted. From Russia he went to Ghent, and there he was instrumental in forging an honorable treaty with Britain.

Adams most admired Gallatin's constant devotion. His tenacity was nowhere more evident than at the beginning of the war, when the work of a decade was in shambles: "With this wound incessantly smarting at his heart; with all his great schemes and brilliant hopes of administrative success shattered . . . , Gallatin was now called upon to take up his burden again and march. He could not escape." Under such circumstances he proved himself the "highest type of practical statesman." Having enough sense to abandon hopeless principles, he did the best he knew how.

Adams mined for his own purposes the story of Gallatin's

life after retirement. The election of Andrew Jackson, Adams charged, put an end to his hero's usefulness. The anti-intellectual Jackson had no interest in a person like Gallatin, nor he for Jackson. The political scene and the rising spirit of crass and grasping materialism appalled him; he lived long enough to witness the total corruption of American life. As usual Gallatin did what he could to set fellow citizens on a truer course, writing a pamphlet in support of the Second Bank of the United States and campaigning constantly against soft money. He thus appeared to anticipate Adams's own concerns over finance.

If Adams found in Gallatin the angel of American politics, he discovered in John Randolph the perfect demon. He had dealt with Randolph occasionally in the Gallatin biography, but he received an opportunity to develop the subject when editor John T. Morse asked him to do a volume for the American Statesmen Series. *John Randolph* appeared in 1882. In Randolph, race, milieu, and time conspired to produce a monster. The Virginia aristocracy into which he was born bred a set of contradictory traits that shocked and irritated the New England Adams. On the one hand Randolph possessed the manners of a gentleman, had strong pride in family and section, and demonstrated an openhanded generosity to everyone he liked. At the same time family ownership of slaves had engendered in him both arrogance and condescension, while Virginia's gentle climate had encouraged sloth and lack of discipline. These contradictions, magnified by an unstable personality, produced an exotic creature, "as pure a Virginian Quixote as ever an American Cervantes could have conceived."

Randolph was bound to oppose the Constitution of 1787: For a man so filled with family and regional pride and so lacking in self-discipline, strong central government was anathema. He became a vigorous states' righter and strict constructionist of the Constitution, but unlike Gallatin he was unable to adjust once circumstances had demolished the Jeffersonian program. To the end of his life he continued to tilt at political windmills.

During the first years of the Jefferson administration, however, Randolph seemed to abandon his creed. A member of the U.S. House and chairman of the Ways and Means Committee, he supported the Louisiana Purchase even though the Constitution had not specifically authorized it. Randolph also favored war against the Spanish when they refused to relinquish Florida, although war would sabotage the Jeffersonian financial program and extend the power of central government. In leading the impeachment fight against Justice Samuel Chase, he abandoned strict constructionism, claiming that the Constitution permitted impeachment for political and not just criminal offenses.

Yet around 1806 Randolph began to rail at Jefferson, Madison, and Gallatin for repudiating their own principles. He loudly proclaimed his independence of the Republican party, voting against the embargo, against the administration's solution to the infamous Yazoo land squabble in Georgia, and against preparations for the War of 1812. He became so vindictive that he opposed the executive on principle, regardless of merit and frequently to the point of contradiction. As he became older and more bitter, his speeches grew increasingly violent, slanderous, and deranged. He would enter the House booted and spurred, riding whip in hand, and proceed to unleash a stream of invective at whomever caught his attention, a performance often assisted by the effects of alcohol.

Randolph resisted every measure of President John Quincy Adams. Besides denouncing internal improvements, he castigated Adams's foreign policy and his secretary of state, Henry Clay. The latter, Randolph accused, had turned his back on his native Kentucky by his advocacy of internal improvements. He once referred to Adams and Clay as "the coalition of Blifil and Black George, — . . . the combination, unheard of till then, of the Puritan with the blackleg." Re-

viling Clay for his crucial support of Adams in the election
of 1828, he lamented that Clay's parents had brought into
the world "this being, so brilliant yet so corrupt, which,
like a rotten mackerel by moonlight, shined and stunk."

These rantings were relatively harmless compared to his
campaign to wed slavery and states' rights. So long as the
South had controlled the central government, Adams remarked, it was content with a strong union. Nor was it the
only section to talk of nullification and secession; at the
Hartford Convention some New England Federalists had
threatened to leave the United States and create a north-
eastern confederacy. Only after the South lost national
dominance did states' rights become its preserve; then what
had been a respectable stance was inextricably bound to
treason and rebellion. And the evil genius of this merger
between states' rights and slavery was John Randolph. Year
after year from the floor of the House he defended the
rights of sovereign southern states to hold and retrieve slaves.
John C. Calhoun took up where Randolph left off, and
when Randolph died in 1833, the stage was set for secession
and civil war.

Taken together the Randolph and Gallatin biographies
presented a clear moral lesson: The American Republic
would succeed only if it could elevate the Gallatins to
public office while steering clear of the Randolphs. Yet both
men were largely the products of forces beyond their control. Gallatin's high ideals, his sense of duty, and his ad-
justment to reality flowed from his upbringing and what
Taine called the "moral temperature" of his age. Randolph
likewise was a creature of personality and environment.

Gallatin clearly represented the statesmanship envisioned
by the Adamses, who believed that the struggle against ignorance and immorality would be arduous. Such dogged-
ness had distinguished the family for three generations. Yet
Henry was unable to follow Gallatin's example. By failing
to work within the possibilities of post–Civil War America,

he cut himself off from any chance of furthering reform. In this respect he resembled the despised Randolph, who also had refused to accept the exigencies of his day. Already Adams had begun to embrace a historical determinism that denied people the free will to alter their surroundings. With the Randolph and Gallatin biographies behind him, Adams was now ready for a larger examination of those forces in the early Republic that had led to the failure of the American experiment.

V

History of the Experiment: Part II

THE HISTORICAL COMMUNITY received the *Life of Albert Gallatin* well and the *Randolph* sold respectably among educated readers. For the most part Adams was blissfully contented, at least on a personal level: He continued to enjoy his rich social life and, absorbed in his work, he overcame much of the old self-doubt. To Henry Cabot Lodge he explained his particular satisfaction in writing. "You know my way of thinking," he told his young correspondent. "I got it from my father, and so I suppose it is merely a piece of hereditary imbecility. . . . At any rate I hold that to be happy in life is possible, so far as depends on oneself, only by being always busily occupied upon objects that seem worth doing. It is the occupation, not the objects, which makes happiness." To friend and confidant Charles Milnes Gaskell he wrote that life had a "summer-like repose about it; a self-contained, irresponsible, devil-may-care indifference to the future . . . ; a feeling that one's bed is made, and one can rest on it till it becomes necessary to go to bed for ever." Adams found comfort, like many middle-aged persons, in sheer productivity. The decision to leave Harvard had cut him off from Boston and had given him a vocation all his own. The first of the Adamses to devote himself to history, he now had established a personal identity. Only his and Marian's inability to have children marred these placid and confident years.

With nothing on the horizon to disturb their snug little paradise, Adams and his wife decided to build their own house on Lafayette Square. Together with John Hay they bought a lot at the corner of 16th and H Streets and commissioned the celebrated architect H. H. Richardson to design adjoining dwellings. Construction began in the summer of 1884.

Adams's sense of peace helped him to maintain some degree of faith in his country's prospects, in spite of his conclusions in the *Gallatin* and *Randolph* volumes. He continued, as if by habit, to cavil at the performance of his neighbors across the square in the White House. His well-meaning old friend James A. Garfield lacked initiative; ex-spoilsman Chester A. Arthur would bring the presidency to new depths of decay. He was pleasantly surprised, however, when Arthur supported and signed the Pendleton Civil Service Act of 1883. At last the federal government had instituted the merit system. Only ten percent of the bureaucracy came under the law initially, but this was a beginning; the reform element seemed to be making a bit of progress against corruption.

All the while Adams was hard at work on his nine-volume *History of the United States of America during the Administrations of Thomas Jefferson and James Madison* (1889–1891). The earlier Gallatin and Randolph studies had confirmed his belief that the Jefferson and Madison years were a watershed in the American experiment. The period was crucial because Jefferson's victory in 1800 permitted a practical test of liberal republicanism after twelve years of Federalist rule. Under Washington and Adams the Federalists had taken a dimmer view of humanity than did Jefferson and his allies, believing that strong central government by the educated and well-to-do was essential to public order and morality. It was also after Jefferson's election that American nationalism was forged, most citizens emerging from the War of 1812 with a clear national identity and a determination to preserve the federal union. In addition, American character crystallized during this period. Still inchoate when Jefferson assumed the presidency, it was well formed by the time Madison retired in 1817.

Before sitting down to write the *History,* Adams embarked upon a thorough research of his subject. He already had used many of the pertinent sources for the *Gallatin* and the *Randolph,* but the *History* required much more digging, particularly into documents in foreign archives. For the history of the country during that time had been affected greatly by European events. He and Marian accordingly spent a year in England and on the Continent, interspersing archival work with sight-seeing, shopping, and theatergoing. Only after returning to Washington in 1880 did the writing begin.

The *History*'s organization was dictated by the tenets of Adam's scientific scholarship and by the requirements of his themes. He spent the initial six chapters and nearly a third of the first volume describing the United States in 1800 and the problems it confronted. The next four thousand pages traced the evolution of these difficulties. Then in the last four chapters of the ninth volume Adams summed up the country's development during the intervening seventeen years, placing particular weight upon the nation's successes and failures in solving the difficulties of 1800.

Want of national unity was high on the list of obstacles. Its initial cause was the country's enormous size coupled with a poor transportation system. Even before the acquisition of the vast Louisiana Territory, Adams pointed out, the distances separating the Atlantic seaboard from the sparse settlements on the trans-Appalachian frontier appeared insurmountable. It took twenty-two days under the best conditions for a letter posted in Washington, D.C., to arrive in Nashville, Tennessee. There was a pressing need for internal improvements, which the federal government alone could afford, but states' rights sentiment and strict constructionism blocked the way.

Provincialism, too, was an impediment to national unity. In the tradition of Buckle and Taine, Adams attributed regional differences partly to geography and climate. The severe weather and rocky soil of New England fostered a ruggedness, a harshness, and an independence unknown elsewhere in the country. The good soil and mild temperatures of the South, by contrast, had bred both indiscipline and warm hospitality and explained further the southerner's agrarian bias. In the middle states a combination of navigable rivers, excellent harbors, and fertile land gave rise to centers of commerce and finance.

Cultural and intellectual factors also influenced development of the three areas. The Puritan settlement of New England accounted for its continuing Calvinistic spirit and for its intolerance. In Pennsylvania religious pluralism and a cosmopolitan population were important factors to the Keystone State's prosperity and political moderation. In Virginia a belief that the population had descended from English Cavaliers resulted in chivalric manners, overweening pride, and contempt for other sections of the country.

Also evident by 1800 was a western sectionalism, likewise derived from nature and history. The Appalachian Range extending from Maine to Georgia placed a barrier between the West and the Atlantic states. All the West's navigable rivers flowed into the Mississippi and thence into the Gulf of Mexico, whereas the waterways of the East emptied into the Atlantic. Cheap and reliable water transportation between the two regions was thus next to impossible. From the East it involved a trip down the Atlantic coast, around the tip of Florida, and through the Gulf to New Orleans.

Cargo and passengers then had to be poled in flatboats up the Mississippi and Ohio rivers. Besides these natural boundaries, frontier hardships had produced a coarse and frequently anti-intellectual type, contemptuous of eastern culture and ideas. Every indication thus pointed to the evolution of several nations; the former British colonies would follow the European example and become a permanent set of squabbling neighbors.

Adams found the matter of American character more difficult to handle because of a lack of trustworthy evidence. He proposed that Americans in 1800 were hardworking and self-reliant, qualities needed to settle a new land. In spite of the trying conditions, people were essentially moral and mild-mannered. A level of prosperity much above the European average and a nearly universal chance to earn a decent living mitigated the viciousness and criminality that sprung from Old World pauperism.

Americans in 1800 were accordingly a simple people who made an adequate if simple living from the soil. However encouraging these characteristics might be to a Jefferson or a Rousseau, they were not calculated to erase the want of nationalism in the United States. Taken together these traits produced a popular conservatism, manifesting itself in anti-intellectual contempt for higher learning, failure to appreciate the fruits of science and technology, widespread ignorance of finance, and maniacal hatred of banks. Yet to overcome provincialism and sectional rivalry, the country required scientific investigation, application of technology to transportation and communication, and the expenditure of many millions on internal improvements. Without them, the hope of extending republican institutions over half a continent was bound to fail.

The three themes of the *History* were intimately related. Democracy could not conquer the country's great expanse without better transportation, which would remain out of reach unless citizens overcame their blindness to science and technology. A European despot might command the building of requisite roads and canals, but American democracy demanded the consent of voters and their representatives. "The task of overcoming popular inertia . . . was new, and seemed to offer peculiar difficulties," wrote Adams. "They could do little without changing their old habit of mind, and without learning to love novelty for novelty's sake."

Nevertheless, the majority of Americans were confident about their experiment. Part of their optimism came from ignorance of the trials confronting them. Much of their cheerfulness, however, derived from belief in human equality and perfectability. Determined "to lift the average man upon an intellectual and social level with the most favored," they staked their country's whole existence upon such a dubious experiment.

Their principal chance of success, Adams believed, lay in a lack of Old World restraint. Ancient customs, rigid class distinctions, heavy taxation, and war had kept most people from realizing their potential for intelligence, goodness, and industry. In the United States few such barriers remained. The American stood "stripped for the hardest work, every muscle firm and elastic, every ounce of brain ready for use, and not a trace of superfluous flesh on his nervous and supple body." Adams found society "so organized as to use its human forces with more economy than could be approached by any society of the world elsewhere."

The official spokesman of this philosophy was Thomas Jefferson, who represented the dreams and aspirations of most Americans. Only die-hard Federalists, those inveterate pessimists and misanthropes, rejected his doctrines. Jefferson's determination as president to put these ideas into practice therefore made the history of his and Madison's administrations a history of the American people from 1800 to 1817.

After setting the stage in the *History,* Adams proceeded

to outline, as he had in the Gallatin and Randolph biographies, the Jeffersonian political philosophy. The new president was bent on sweeping away the last vestiges of Old World restraint, leaving citizens free to expend their benign and constructive energies. This meant that Jefferson had to dismantle entirely the Federalist political machine, with its loose constructionism, its centralizing tendencies, its internal taxes and perpetual debts, and its standing army and navy. Readers of the *Gallatin* and *Randolph* already knew that Jefferson and Madison would fail. But in the *History* Adams told the story more agonizingly, never missing a shred of proof or an opportunity to show how the Jeffersonians ended up behaving like Federalists.

After chronicling the successes of Jefferson during the initial years of his first term, Adams took up the earliest major threat to the Republican school, the Louisiana Purchase. The crisis was partially the effect of geography. New Orleans was crucial to western farmers who floated their produce down the Mississippi and then transshipped it to ports on the East Coast or in Europe. When Spain revoked the right to deposit goods in New Orleans, westerners demanded action from Washington. Under the circumstances Jefferson offered to buy the city and its immediate environs from the French, who recently had reclaimed it. Napoleon offered to sell the entire Louisiana Territory instead. Since the Constitution was silent on the matter of buying land from a foreign power, the president had qualms about the deal and for a time urged a constitutional amendment to legitimize it. Republicans in both House and Senate refused to hear of an amendment and justified the transaction with old Federalist arguments: The purchase was in the general welfare, it was necessary and proper to the common defense, it was essential to continued national prosperity, and it fell within the treaty-making power of the president and the Senate.

Swallowing his hesitations, Jefferson accepted supporters'

arguments and acquired the new domain. Adams considered this action every bit as disgraceful as that of the worst European tyrant. The president occupied a land whose inhabitants had not consented to transfer to a foreign jurisdiction. To add to the ignominy, Jefferson then appointed a governor who ruled Louisiana for several years without any representative institutions. The citizens of the territory were taxed and governed without their consent by a country that gave them no voice in their government. The author of the Declaration of Independence now found himself in the position of George III.

Next followed Jefferson's attack on the Federalist bench. He regarded the Federalists with whom John Adams had packed the national judiciary as the last barriers to complete Republican triumph. Accordingly, he urged the House of Representatives to launch impeachment proceedings against several federal judges. Not only did the House's attempt to indict Justice Samuel Chase without proof of criminal wrongdoing involve a loose construction of the Constitution, but the failure to convict him on purely political grounds meant that Federalist-dominated courts would remain inviolable. Chief Justice John Marshall, made secure by the unsuccessful attack on the courts, went on to build an indestructible body of precedent in defense of strong central government. In their ill-advised campaign against Chase, Republicans had helped defeat their own creed.

Jefferson's high-handed tactics in trying to wrest Florida from Spain also accorded badly with his doctrines. As much as possible he conducted negotiations without the advice of the Senate, expecting it to ratify his arrangements without demur. Again, his conduct was reminiscent of Europe's divine right monarchs.

Adams already had narrated the whole embargo morass in the *Gallatin* and added little to this story in the *History*. Attempts to coerce Britain and France through trade restrictions were doomed from the outset, and Madison's decision to go to war in 1812 was the crowning blow to Republican designs. The failures of Jefferson and Madison were due mainly to their naive trust in human nature: Only war could force Britain to respect the United States and unify its people. Thus circumstances and not theories had dictated their course. In one of the most eloquent passages of the *History* Adams wrote, "The workings of human development were never more strikingly shown than in the helplessness with which the strongest political and social forces in the world followed or resisted at haphazard the necessities of a movement which they could not control or comprehend." The great powers and their leaders "were borne away by the stream, struggling, gesticulating, praying, murdering, robbing; each blind to everything but a selfish interest, and all helping more or less unconsciously to reach the new level which society was obliged to seek."

Besides reciting in detail the Jeffersonian desertion of principle, Adams took every chance to point out instances of incompetence or corruption in the two administrations. High on the list was the Burr conspiracy. According to Adams, Jefferson himself shared part of the blame for Aaron Burr's treasonable designs. By siding against Burr in the political fights of New York state, the president forced him into the arms of dissatisfied Federalists. They wanted Burr to lead New York out of the Union and into a confederacy with New England. When this failed, Burr allegedly had plotted to conquer Mexico, to seize the Louisiana Territory, and to make himself emperor of both. Burr's machinations revealed that some Americans were not above the lowest political intrigues and in this regard did not differ from their European counterparts.

The near treasonable activities of the Essex Junto and Hartford Convention were no more uplifting. The former, taking its name from Essex County, Massachusetts, contained men reputed to be among New England's most intel-

ligent and public-spirited: Timothy Pickering, Theodolphus
Parsons, Fisher Ames, and Stephen Higginson. Hating Jeffersonian democracy and convinced that Federalism was
dying, they wished to make the entire Northeast independent. There they might preserve order, intelligence, and
morality from the anarchy, ignorance, and brutality of the
democratic masses. Their early calculations came to nothing, but when the War of 1812 began, they and others of
their persuasion used New England discontent as a pretext
to call a convention at Hartford, Connecticut. They protested Madison's ineptitude and threatened secession if the
war dragged on. That such men, lauded for their probity
and reason, should behave in this way was one more blow
to the Jeffersonian faith in human nature. "The representatives of the wise and good looked at politics with eyes which
saw no farther than those of the most profligate democrat
into the morality of the game."

The quality of federal legislators also disgusted Adams.
Political interests alone motivated them and few had the
background and mind to legislate wisely. Adams already had
described in detail the House's refusal to take Gallatin's
advice on war preparations, on paying for the War of 1812,
and on rechartering the First Bank. The House's vacillation
on what to do about the continuing French and British
violations of American neutral rights further revealed its
inadequacy.

Madison's management of the War of 1812 was yet another instance of incompetence and political jobbery. Cabinet positions were assigned for political reasons, Secretary
of War Eustis being one of the more blatant examples.
Officers in the field were for the most part equally amateur-
ish, and the militiamen upon whom the government depended fled more frequently than they fought. The government was unable even to defend Washington. When the
British attacked, Madison had to flee to the Maryland
woods, helpless to prevent the torching of his capital. Only

the country's swift and maneuverable ships saved it from complete humiliation.

When Madison left office in 1817, it was clear to any honest person that the Republican experiment lay in shambles. The two Republican presidents had aimed to reveal the basic goodness and intelligence of the people, but ultimately they had to abandon all their doctrines. At the end of their terms it was impossible to see how they differed in practice from the staunchest Federalists. Equally demoralizing had been the conspiracies against the Union, the constant political intriguing, and the incompetence of many elected officials. Jefferson and Madison had placed too high an estimate upon the people's abilities. In reality Americans were little different from their European cousins. They had not overcome the bonds of human nature and had to face the future knowing that they "must bear the common burdens of humanity."

Throughout the nine volumes of the *History* as well as in the Gallatin and Randolph biographies, Adams had been hard on Jefferson and Madison and their doctrines. Occasionally, he took iconoclastic delight in pointing out the failures and inconsistencies of the great figures of the early Republic. Nevertheless, he sympathized with them and their programs and would have applauded their success. He had complete contempt for their extremist opponents, the Essex Junto and the leaders of the Hartford Convention. Indeed, just before leaving Harvard, Adams had edited a work entitled *Documents of New England Federalism* (1877) in which he collected and presented all the available evidence to damage the reputation of the "high Federalists" whom his great-grandfather John Adams had despised.

Adams did not leave readers of the *History* on an entirely negative note. Surprisingly, he noted, the country had emerged from the War of 1812 with a strong sense of national unity. The conflict brought the American people together, and they could take pride in having survived a second clash with the most powerful kingdom in the world. They bragged about their superb ships and the overwhelming victory at New Orleans. In addition, disloyal Federalists who had protested the war and toyed with secession so discredited themselves that the party disintegrated within a couple of years. Even after the resurgence of a viable two-party system, nationalism remained, potent enough to sustain the country through disunion and civil war two generations later. In fact, Americans proved so devoted to the Union that North and South patched up their quarrel almost as soon as the matter of slavery was settled.

Another result of the War of 1812 was the solidification of American character. The great energy and independence remained, as did the comparative lack of depravity and vicious crime. And in spite of the hatred against Great Britain, Americans still wished to avoid Europe's conflicts. The people had lost much of their backwardness, at least regarding science and technology. Whereas they had ridiculed John Fitch's crude steamboat of the 1780s, they welcomed Robert Fulton's model and generally recognized the need for extensive internal improvements. The war's fiscal difficulties also convinced most that a sound banking system was needed for the country's prosperity, and in 1816 Congress created the Second Bank of the United States. If Americans were basically no more moral or intelligent than Europeans, they were beginning to exhibit a greater practicality and flexibility and seemed willing to tap all the resources of the human intellect if they could foresee tangible results. Still, Adams wondered if these results would save the American experiment, and he closed his narrative with a series of questions about the future: "What interests were to vivify a society so vast and uniform? What ideals were to ennoble it? What object, besides physical content, must a democratic continent aspire to attain?"

Time alone held the answers. Adams already had considered much of the subsequent evolution of the American experiment. Writing the life story of Albert Gallatin, who died in 1849, had led Adams thirty years beyond the Jefferson and Madison administrations. His articles and reviews had covered the events of the 1860s and 1870s, and in searching for the causes of contemporary problems, he frequently had referred to the 1850s. But Adam's most significant comments on the national experiment in his own generation appeared in the novel *Democracy* (1880). The work was an exposé of Washington politics, and in it Adams dwelt on some of the same ideas treated in the *History*.

Just when this project took form is impossible to determine. As a child reading Charles Dickens, Adams became aware of the power of fiction, and in adulthood he savored the political novels of Anthony Trollope. Like many writers of nonfiction, he may have wished to try his hand at the novel, seeing it as the ultimate act of literary creation.

The story's protagonist is Mrs. Madeleine Lee, a thirty-year-old widow who flees New York City to find new meaning for her empty life. Neither charitable work nor serious reading and study have consoled her in the loss of both husband and son. She moves to Washington with her younger, unmarried sister, hoping to find some purpose to existence by observing and becoming part of the workings of American politics. Madeleine's quest is, in reality, that of the author. She wants to get at the heart of the political system, to grasp its philosophical basis as well as its practical operation in order to see how well it has measured up to the dreams of the founders.

The sisters make an easy entry into Washington society with the help of John Carrington, a distant cousin who resides in the capital, and he makes sure that they receive invitations from all the right people. In no time the sisters establish a fashionable salon in their house on Lafayette Square. Among their guests are Silas P. Ratcliffe, senator from Illinois; Nathan Gore, former minister to Spain; C. C.

French, a young reform-minded congressman; Hartbeest Schneidkoupon, a wealthy tariff lobbyist; Baron Jacobi, a cynical old Bulgarian diplomat; Lord Skye, the British minister to Washington; charming, acid-tongued socialite Victoria Dare; and, of course, Carrington. Ratcliffe, who also has lost his spouse, falls in love with Mrs. Lee, who has encouraged his attentions in order to gain access to the centers of power. For Mrs. Lee, Ratcliffe personifies the American political system: He has risen from humble midwestern origins to become a leading voice in the Senate and a prospective presidential candidate. His rise is the embodiment of the American dream.

All too quickly the dream becomes a nightmare. Madeleine finds herself falling in love with Ratcliffe, but at the same time she begins to have doubts about his integrity. When she asks him why he does not press harder for reform, he answers that he can go no further than his constituents will allow, that the majority are content with the status quo. Such discussions occur more and more frequently. During one of them, the worldly wise Baron Jacobi asks what all the fuss is about; he cannot understand why so many Americans continue to insist that they are more moral than the rest of humanity. "You Americans believe yourselves to be excepted from the operation of general laws." Finding Washington as corrupt as any capital in the Old World, he has difficulty fathoming their innocence. And he expects the situation to grow worse. Before long "the United States will . . . be more corrupt than Rome under Caligula; more corrupt than the Church under Leo X; more corrupt than France under the Regent."

Shaken by Jacobi's harangue, Madeleine demands to know of her other guests if the baron is correct. Nathan Gore tries to evade the question, but Madeleine will not give up. She has to know "whether America is right or wrong." If the country is exactly like any other, the founders' experiment is doomed. Gore answers that one must have faith in the

American people and their system, and that democracy is the last hope for human happiness, because it "asserts the fact that the masses are now raised to higher intelligence than formerly." "All our civilization," he adds, "aims at this mark. . . . I myself want to see the result. I grant it is an experiment, but it is the only direction society can take that is worth its taking."

Meanwhile Carrington has been keeping a secret that will force Madeleine to make up her mind about both Ratcliffe and the American experiment. A Mrs. Baker had employed Carrington to handle the estate of her dead husband, a notorious lobbyist; Carrington finds in his papers a document showing that Senator Ratcliffe had taken $50,000 from a steamship company for supporting a subsidy bill. When Madeleine is about to marry Ratcliffe in spite of her doubts, Carrington exposes the senator's wrongdoing. Utterly crushed, she refuses his proposal. No small part of her misery results from knowing that she was compromised by the political system. She has flirted with the senator in order to reach the inner sanctum. At last she has "got to the bottom of this business of democratic government" only to discover that it was "nothing more than government of any other kind." The American people and their politics were no better and no worse than any other people and system; the country was not exempt from the laws of nature.

Democracy became a sensation overnight, going through several printings immediately. Reformers exulted that the author had hit the mark exactly and scandalmongers were euphoric. Because the characters were thinly veiled versions of real men and women, readers speculated endlessly on who they were. It took little imagination to guess that Ratcliffe resembled James G. Blaine, widely suspected of taking bribes while a congressman. Carrington bore a likeness to Clarence King. Jacobi was probably Turkish Minister Aristarchi Bey, while Gore was no doubt John Lothrop Motley, a New England historian and diplomat. Since Adams used actual personalities as models, he insisted that the publishers not name him as author, and thus readers also speculated about the book's writer. Some supposed it was John Hay or Clarence King, while others guessed it was Marian. Only one or two suspected Adams himself.

It is clear that *Democracy* recapitulated the conclusions to which Adams came in his historical works. Madeleine Lee is aware that the American people are not selecting wise and virtuous men to lead them. There are too many Randolphs and not enough Gallatins in government. She also doubts that Americans are any more capable of enlightened rule than others in the world, a proposition that Adams put forth in the *History* as well as in the two biographies.

The writings of the Washington years thus sounded a single message. A study of the past demonstrated that the American people had not lived up to the hopes of the more sanguine founders. Still, Adams did not despair completely. He congratulated fellow citizens in the *History* for overcoming their popular conservatism and for surmounting the barriers to full nationhood. And in the final chapters of the *History,* the latest of all his writings during this period, he cautioned readers against making rash conclusions about the future.

VI

America Comes of Age

ON DECEMBER 6, 1885, Adams received a shock that sent him reeling back into the present. His wife committed suicide. Marian had suffered deep depression since her father's death in the spring, yet by early December she seemed much better, and Adams was encouraged. Perhaps her improvement stemmed from the peace that comes when a person decides to escape his or her misery once and for all. Whatever the case, Henry went out for a short walk and returned to find her dead. She had swallowed some developing chemicals from the darkroom she used as an amateur photographer. In the following weeks he refused to speak of her unless absolutely necessary and refrained from doing so until the weeks became months and the months became years.

In his mourning Adams commissioned Augustus Saint-Gaudens to design a memorial sculpture for Marian's grave in Washington's Rock Creek Cemetery. He wanted the memorial to evoke the peace of the Orient, as represented by the Kwanon Buddha. The result was disappointing. Above his wife's remains he found a seated bronze woman wholly Western in appearance. The figure also lacked the delicacy Adams had wished; the arms and legs abnormally

large and the facial features coarse. Still, the total effect was
one of peaceful resignation. Adams spent long hours sitting
on a marble bench opposite the shrouded form and took
comfort from the knowledge that Marian rested beneath
his feet.

The *History*'s reception did little to cheer the widower.
He had hoped to become another George Bancroft, but
Bancroft's multivolume history was patriotic and romantic,
giving it a wider, more popular appeal. Adams had produced a scholarly work for which the general public had
small appetite. Sales of only a few thousand sets were discouraging. He again saw himself as a failure and lamented
that he could not measure up to family standards. His
father's death in 1886 and his mother's in 1889 caused him
to think a great deal about the family and his place in it,
and these reflections intensified his self-doubts. The confidence and contentment of the Washington years vanished.
Sheer duty forced him to finish the *History*, and for the
sake of internal consistency he tried not to let his mood
color its conclusions unduly.

Once he had completed the *History*, however, Adams felt
free to project his own unhappiness upon the rest of the
world. As time passed he became more pessimistic and de-
terministic. Reiterating and extending the charge he had
made in the *History* — that Americans were not exempt
from the general laws of human nature — he saw his country's development as part of a general decline in Western
civilization. Severe economic depression and the nation's
emergence as a world power were significant manifestations
of this demise. He wakened to the first abruptly in the summer of 1893 while visiting his friends the Camerons in
Switzerland. There an urgent telegram from brother Charles
filled him with alarm. The stock market had crashed, banks
had folded by the hundreds, and the family finances were
in danger; Henry was needed right away.

The picture was grim when he reached Quincy in early

August. His three brothers had gathered at the family home for a council of war. John, who had been managing the family trust, was on the verge of a nervous breakdown; he would die a year later. Charles, failing to secure credit for the Union Pacific, already had lost control of the railroad, and his vast real estate holdings in the West were threatened. Brooks was sure that the entire economy was beyond recovery. Henry immediately joined the feverish attempts to keep the family afloat financially, sharing what he had learned from supervising his own ample investments. Together they saved the family trust through a series of retrenchments and economies.

The fear and uncertainty at Quincy were duplicated in millions of homes throughout the land. During the next four years of depression there would be massive unemployment and bankruptcy in the worst economic collapse the United States had known. Ironically, the acuteness of the panic resulted in part from the unprecedented growth of the American economy during the previous quarter of a century. Since the Civil War, the nation had become an industrial giant. War itself had stimulated northern industry, permitting factory owners to save large amounts of capital and to launch even greater enterprises in peacetime. Population had doubled from 31 million in 1860 to 62 million in 1890. Over 10 million immigrants had poured into the United States during the same period, and they as well as the native born reared large families. The population increase fed the hunger of factories, mills, and mines for labor, while ensuring a rising demand for goods and services. Better and more powerful steam engines, an expanding railroad network, the invention of the telegraph and telephone, and the constant stream of new industrial machinery produced the most productive and efficient industrial plant on earth. By 1900 the nation led the world in the production of iron and steel.

A downturn in the economy now was bound to be worse

than it had ever been before. The dependence of many more Americans upon industrial jobs in cities meant greater unemployment than in the past. When production slowed or when factories closed, men lost their livelihoods. Earlier depressions had caused hardships, but in a largely agrarian population the crises were not so acute, since the farmer usually could remain on the land and at least put food on the table.

The economic revolution also had given birth to great corporations. Although their owners extolled the virtues of competition, they did everything they could to destroy it and seize control of entire markets. Workers in these large firms were powerless to redress low wages and poor conditions. In the cities unhealthy, degrading slums arose at alarming rates. Industrialization even had a disruptive effect upon agriculture, for the new farm technology resulted in overproduction and low prices. Rapid expansion in both agriculture and industry demonstrated as well the continuing need for a more flexible money supply. The depression underlined these problems and dramatized pitfalls in the American economic and social systems.

For Adams the panic was fresh evidence that the American experiment was in serious difficulty. His brother Brooks agreed. Up to this time Henry had not been particularly close to his younger brother. Brooks had graduated from Harvard, had practiced law, and like his older brothers, had contributed to the periodical press on a variety of subjects. By the eighties he had focused his interest on history. His *Emancipation of Massachusetts* (1887) had debunked the state's Puritan tradition and had angered conservatives. When Henry returned to Quincy in the summer of 1893, he discovered Brooks working on a manuscript later published as *The Law of Civilization and Decay* (1895). It was basically an economic interpretation of Western civilization, which the author enriched with insights from the panic. Henry was fascinated by his brother's ideas, although he

did not concur on every interpretation. The two debated
the summer away in a storm of intellectual excitement. So
enthralled were they with their bold speculations that they
nearly forgot their recent brush with financial ruin. For the
rest of their lives they maintained a spirited exchange of
ideas.

In his *Civilization and Decay* Brooks advanced a thesis
that buttressed Henry's doubts about the United States and
the Western world as a whole. The West had endured re-
current economic crises, each of which had a ripple effect
upon other aspects of life. The crises were more severe over
time, and in the end Brooks predicted that civilization
would crumble under the stress. At the heart of these economic shocks was the law of concentration. The law assumed fear and greed to be the prime motives in human
behavior; people feared one another and the unfathomable
forces around them. In response to their anxieties they tried
to concentrate as much power as possible as a means of
protection. The three principal varieties of power were religious, military, and commercial, forms corresponding to
stages of cultural development. During each stage life took
its overall tone from the prevailing type of power. Primitive
societies relied heavily upon religious authority. Later ones
placed trust in the military, and at a more advanced stage
they invested most of their energies in commerce.

Since the Renaissance the West had been in a commercial
stage; the capitalist rather than the warrior or the priest
dominated life. War and religion by no means disappeared,
but capitalists used both for their own purposes. The
wealthy bought priests, soldiers, and politicians and dictated government policy. The capitalist paid writers and
thinkers to praise the system and bribed the clergy to preach
a gospel of wealth to the successful and a doctrine of submission to the poor. As patron of the arts, the capitalist exploited and debased aesthetic tastes.

Brooks admitted in his writings that he borrowed heavily

from Comte. He also confessed that his economic determinism had an ally in Karl Marx. Neither Henry nor Brooks had any sympathy with the bulk of Marx's writings, but his philosophy of history engrossed them. As Henry put it, "I never struck a book [*Capital*] which taught me so much, and with which I disagreed so radically in conclusion." His pessimistic soul rejected, among other things, Marx's vision of a proletarian paradise.

If Henry and Brooks could not share the Marxian utopia, they did concur that there was a limit to commercial concentration. The capitalist's rapacity was unlimited. In his quest for riches, however, he created serious social, economic, and political dislocations that would destroy the modern commercial order. Henry and Brooks were convinced that capitalists already had pushed Western commercial society to the point of upheaval and self-destruction. Two practices were particularly dangerous and both aimed at economic concentration. One was the insincere espousal of unlimited competition; the other was the attempt to restrict the money supply. Demanding and obtaining freedom from state interference, capitalists succeeded in ruining weaker competitors. The restricted money supply deprived small and aspiring entrepreneurs of funds with which to challenge big business.

A clear contradiction was evident between the capitalists' cry for free competition and their efforts to destroy it. Increasingly severe panics and untold misery would lead either to revolution or to total economic collapse. In either situation society might revert to a primitive condition. In the summer of 1893 the two brothers believed such a catastrophe was near. Even after the depression had run its course, they did not change their minds, admonishing that the last and final crash was just around the corner. Henry's letters raged against the agents of decline, the bankers and entrepreneurs. To Charles Milnes Gaskell he complained of the prestige and political weight of the newly rich and their lackeys:

"George M. Pullman and Andrew Carnegie and Grover Cleveland are our Crassus and Pompey and Caesar, — our proud American triumvirate, the types of our national mind and ideals. We are under a sort of terror before them." To another correspondent he declared, "We are under the whip of the bankers."

Much of Adam's anger originated in his disgust for materialism, be it philosophical or pecuniary, for materialism obstructed the path of ideals. Too often selfishness and greed blocked moral progress. Without higher aspirations the American experiment was doomed to miscarry, one of its mainstays having been an acceptance of absolute truths. So long as Americans held to their idealism, to their reliance upon wisdom and virtue, there was hope. As Adams saw it, modern materialism now threatened to obliterate all idealism.

Yet there was more to Adams's loathing of the *nouveaux riches* than their greed. Like many proper Bostonians, he despised them on principle. While well-to-do New Englanders had made money in commerce and even in industry, they had done so at an earlier period. Their descendants had had the leisure to obtain education and polish and did not spend money in ostentatious display, as did the newly wealthy. More importantly, the true gentleman displayed a strong sense of *noblesse oblige,* a quality not always present in the modern entrepreneur. The fact that many Americans idolized the "captains of industry," while ignoring the steady and sober competence of the old elite, galled Adams and his class.

Big business was not the only quarter from which his class felt threatened. They feared that a rising tide of immigrants from southern and eastern Europe, along with the older Irish Catholics, would destroy national character. Many of them accepted the myth of Protestant, Anglo-Saxon preeminence. And even if they did not believe in their innate superiority, they doubted that the Russian Jew or the

Irish and Italian Catholic could share a culture born of
Protestant England.

In their uneasiness over both the upstart businessman
and the immigrant, many older Americans discovered a
scapegoat in the Jew. The eastern European Jew personified
the supposedly unassimilable character of recent arrivals.
When it came to describing the entrepreneur, they drew
upon the medieval Jewish merchant. The stereotyped Jewish immigrant and trader served as a convenient symbol for
all the patrician loathed. Unfortunately, Adams succumbed
to this "genteel anti-Semitism." Twenty years earlier he had
made anti-Semitic innuendoes against Jay Gould. In the fall
of 1893, while shaking from the threat to family finances, he
returned to the theme of Shylock. To John Hay he wrote,
"If a Rothschild . . . is, by hazard, to be hung up to a lamp-
post, one young and sprightly man named Adams would
like to pull on the rope." Three years later he complained
to Gaskell, "We are in the hands of the Jews. They can do
what they please with our [money] values." When he learned
of the Dreyfus affair in France, Adams leaned strongly
toward the anti-Semitic camp and berated the Jews for
many of France's ills.

In spite of his diatribes, it is difficult to believe that
Adams subscribed to the myth of a worldwide Jewish conspiracy, as did some on both sides of the Atlantic. Rather,
the word *Jew* was for Adams, and for many others of his
class, a convenient term for anything distasteful. His resentment of the businessman and the immigrant arose partly
from a sense of declining class prestige. Wide adulation of
the entrepreneur and massive immigration from southern
and eastern Europe increased the patrician's insecurity.

Adams, however, had no specific remedies for the nation's
troubles. He exhibited no real understanding of the unem-
ployed industrial worker, the debt-ridden farmer, or the
exploited immigrant. Even if he had felt more empathy,

Brooks's law had convinced him that nothing could be done. Hence he had no time for reformers, either for the Populists of the nineties or for the progressives of the twentieth century. Having despaired of remaking his compatriots, he had nothing but scorn for ameliorators. Then, too, the new reform tenets differed from those he had held a generation before. Adams had relied primarily upon moral outrage; the Populists and progressives included plans for state regulation.

Only in his approach to the presidential election of 1896 did Adams make an attempt at practicality. Since his participation in the Liberal Republican and independent movements of the seventies, he had continued in the mugwump tradition, refusing to be loyal to either major party. In 1880 he voted for Republican James A. Garfield, a mild reformer and a friend from free-lance days. The election of 1884 found him siding with Democrat Grover Cleveland against Republican James G. Blaine. Cleveland's advocacy of lower tariffs and his honesty were attractive in contrast to Blaine's reputation for corruption. Adams stayed with Cleveland, who was defeated, in 1888. Four years later he concluded that Republican Benjamin Harrison had performed well and he supported his reelection. In the election of 1896, however, he had difficulty making up his mind between Republican William McKinley and Democrat William Jennings Bryan.

To the electorate the candidates were leagues apart. The charismatic Bryan denounced the agents of economic tyranny; at the Democratic convention he compared the dispossessed farmer and wage earner to a crucified Christ. He called for initiative, referendum, and recall; direct election of senators; open primaries; a federal income tax; more effective railroad regulation; and easier credit for farmers and banking reform. But he placed the most emphasis upon the free and unlimited coinage of silver. The gold standard was the capitalist's main weapon of oppression, and like Henry and Brooks Adams, he believed that bankers had conspired to restrict the money supply.

By contrast, McKinley seemed the epitome of middle-class solidity. As a member of the U.S. House he had upheld protective tariffs and sound money, and he reiterated these stands in 1896. High tariffs would stimulate American business, benefiting employer and employee alike. A gold standard would guarantee monetary stability and economic growth.

The campaign proved the most passionate since 1860. Bryan's followers hailed him as a savior whose election would usher in an age of justice and equality. But to Republicans Bryan was a dangerous radical who would undermine order, decency, and honor. To his advocates McKinley represented dignity and respectability, while Bryanites considered him an errand boy for "gold-bug" capitalists.

Adams was much too sophisticated to be overly excited about the campaign. Yet the idea of free silver attracted him, for free silver might produce inflation and threaten the money lords. Creditors would have to accept payment in devalued currency and would find it harder to manipulate the money supply. For the time being Americans might slow the concentration of capital, saving the country a bit longer from collapse. But the impish side of Adams delighted in the thought of an economic Armageddon: A vote for McKinley could accelerate the decline. He finally decided to cast his lot with McKinley and help seal the Republic's fate. He advised John Hay and brother Brooks to do likewise. Such ethereal speculations were reminiscent of those he and Charles had made in their 1876 article on the Hayes-Tilden contest. They also were typical of the mugwump's frequently unrealistic attitude toward politics. At the same time, Adams's 1896 calculations were made somewhat tongue in cheek. It may be that he voted for McKinley simply because he thought him the more capable man.

The leading issues of the campaign gave slight hint that the United States would emerge an international power within two years. The same economic forces that had produced depression and Bryan's demands for reform were propelling the country into a world arena. Rapid growth of industry and population gave Americans the potential for extraordinary military and diplomatic clout. And many could not wait for the nation to flex its young muscles. Some, like Theodore Roosevelt, wanted to enhance American prestige abroad. Others called for a colonial empire in order to expand trade and thus bring about future prosperity. Champions of Anglo-Saxon superiority such as Reverend Josiah Strong asserted that it was the right and duty of the United States to aid England in uplifting the more benighted peoples of the globe. An American empire would assist the spread of English-speaking civilization.

Most of Adams's fellow mugwumps, Carl Schurz and E. L. Godkin among them, took a dim view of American imperialism. When the United States declared war on Spain in 1898 and then proposed to annex Puerto Rico and the Philippines, mugwumps led the fight against empire. For them colonialism was another betrayal of American ideals; colonies violated both the letter and spirit of the Declaration of Independence. To conquer the Filipinos and Puerto Ricans, who never had had political or cultural ties to the United States, was more reprehensible than what England had done before 1776. The vast majority of American settlers had been willing subjects of the crown and rebelled only after they perceived that king and Parliament had abused their rights. Mugwump hatred of the modern capitalist also contributed to their anti-imperialism. Cries for overseas markets were further examples of unending cupidity: colonialism proved that commercial interests had bought government and forced it to do their bidding. The mugwump position proceeded as well from racial prejudice. If the United States were to take Puerto Rico and the Philippines, the country would expose its racial stock to pollution from alien peoples.

Adams came to share the mugwump conviction that imperialism prostituted the principles of American political and constitutional life. But before reaching that conclusion he began his last idealistic crusade, a campaign to free Cuba from Spain's senile embrace. For a moment it looked as if Adams had regained his most optimistic faith in the American experiment. His interest in Cuba's plight dated from a visit to the island with Clarence King in January 1894. He had become enamored of its tropical beauty during his first trip in 1888 and thereafter tried to spend a portion of each winter there. During the 1894 visit King, who had a knack of getting along with the native population wherever he went, made acquaintances among Cuban revolutionaries. First King and then Adams adopted their cause.

When rebellion broke out in Cuba in 1895, Adams supported it warmly. He declared that the United States should recognize the rebels, assist them financially, and apply diplomatic pressures on Spain to relinquish control. He did not expect that the Spanish, who were in no condition to fight anyone, would declare war on the United States. In Washington he attempted to persuade everyone he knew in government to adopt his plan or something like it. Many agreed with him, including Senator Cameron and Senator John Sherman, both members of the Foreign Relations Committee and the latter its chairman. The senators were so pleased with Adams's arguments on behalf of Cuba that they asked him to draft a committee report urging recognition of Cuban independence. Not satisfied with his efforts, Adams opened his house to two Cuban conspirators, Gonzolo de Quesada and Horatio Rubens, helping them to obtain the ear of official Washington.

Although House and Senate passed resolutions calling for recognition, President Cleveland insisted upon strict neutrality. Furious, Adams denounced Cleveland as a coward and a "fat-headed sculpin." Adams could only hope that an aroused citizenry might force the government's hand. The explosion of the battleship *Maine* in Havana Harbor in February 1898 was just the incident to galvanize public opinion behind independence. President McKinley bowed to popular desire and asked for war against Spain.

Once war commenced Adams wanted it to end quickly and on generous terms for Spain. He wrote to his friend John Hay, now ambassador to Great Britain, about his ideas for peace. Spain should give Cuba her freedom and should extend home rule to Puerto Rico. This accomplished, he wanted no more, for the United States had gone to war to liberate Cuba. When the peace treaty annexed Puerto Rico and the Philippines, Adams was appalled. His country, he wrote Elizabeth Cameron, was a "domineering tyrant." He was even more upset when the Filipinos revolted against annexation. The subsequent war of repression was "contrary to every profession or so-called principle of our lives and history." He added, "I turn green in bed at midnight if I think of the horror of . . . warfare in the Philippines."

Much as he despised the war of subjugation and much as he saw the annexations as a betrayal of the Republic's ideals, Adams could not conceive of turning back. The Spanish were finished in the Caribbean and in the Pacific. If the United States did not enter the void opened by Spain's retreat, some other government would and to the detriment of American interests. The country's wealth and population had pushed it onto a world stage, and no one could reverse the process. Nations always used their potential; such was the law of human nature. To a friend Adams wrote, "If we can pull out of . . . the Philippines, we shall avoid some bad risks. I hope we may. . . . But a political situation is always stronger than all the wishes and wisdom of man." He acknowledged to another correspondent, "I should be glad to see the [peace] Treaty rejected if it would get us out of the Philippines, but the country is big, and our energies vast, and, sooner or later, to the East we must go, for a situation is always stronger than man's will."

The United States would never be the same again and Adams knew it. A century and a quarter after throwing off British rule, the American people became colonial masters themselves. No longer could they claim to be a City on a Hill; no longer were they under a new dispensation releasing them from the evils of the Old World — if, indeed, they ever had been. Adams was sorely disappointed, but he joined no strident protests as did other mugwumps. For him the blow was not so severe. He already had discovered in writing the *History* that force of circumstance was stronger than the best human intentions. The failure of Jeffersonian Republicanism proved this if nothing else did.

Not surprisingly, Adams greeted the twentieth century with deep foreboding, particularly in foreign affairs. Yet his somber mood was not unmixed with pride. The United States had fulfilled John Adams's prophecy that the country would surpass Great Britain in wealth and strength. His great-grandson Henry could not help boasting about the nation's spectacular success in a letter to Brooks in February 1900. After having spent six months in Europe, he had arrived in New York and was immediately "conscious of a change of scale." The people, he added, appear "to sling at least twice the weight, twice as rapidly, and with only half the display of effort.... The sense of energy is overpowering."

At the same time he recognized that the era of pretending that the rest of the world did not exist was gone forever. Since the War of 1812, Americans had been able to act as if they did in fact stand apart from Europe. Such a position had been possible largely because England and the Continent witnessed no major wars that might have involved the United States. But economic and political conditions would no longer allow the country to keep the rest of the world at arm's length. Wherever trouble broke out, American interests were likely to be involved. The nation had to be on guard against potential crises and had to develop a world policy.

Adams was full of speculations about troublesome areas and the menace they posed. He worried constantly, sharing his fear with anyone who would listen. His favorite confidant was Hay, who had been promoted to secretary of state. Indeed, the two old friends chatted daily about foreign affairs whenever both were in Washington. At approximately four o'clock each afternoon Hay would come across Lafayette Square from the old State Department building, gathering up Adams for an hour's stroll. In the course of their wanderings the secretary aired his thoughts and often solicited his companion's reactions. At five they commonly returned to Hay's house for tea.

Hay, who was much less pessimistic about foreign affairs than Adams, was amused and occasionally bored by his friend's dire predictions. Adams sniffed danger everywhere, but particularly in central and eastern Europe and in the Far East. In Europe the troublemakers were Germany and Russia. He feared Russia's latent might, with its abundant natural resources. Competent government and rapid industrialization could transform the Russian Bear into a formidable threat. Russia needed a thorough revolution to shake its lethargy, and such an outcome probably would convulse half the world, as France's revolution had done in 1789. He warned Brooks, "Russia is omnipotence.... I fear Russia much!" To Elizabeth Cameron he wrote, Russia "dwarfs Europe instantly.... I am half crazy with fear that Russia is sailing straight into another French revolution which may upset all Europe and us too."

Disturbing though the prospect was in Russia, Adams suspected that Germany was a more immediate danger to international peace and stability. Sitting astride Europe, the newly formed Reich was a veritable "powder magazine." The blusterings of Kaiser Wilhelm, the arms race with her neighbors, the solidifying alliance system, and the open German sympathy with the Boers in South Africa all convinced Adams that a conflict was probable. War in Europe had to affect the United States economically and diplomatically. American foreign policy should try to foster peace in Europe, and that required an Atlantic alliance with Great Britain and France.

In Asia and the western Pacific Adams worried about the continuing friction between Russia and Japan. Having taken the Philippines, the United States must be more concerned about the balance of arms in the Pacific. The State Department should try to maintain a stalemate between Russia and Japan so that neither could dominate China or threaten the Philippines. Adams applauded Hay's and President Roosevelt's successful arbitration of the Russo-Japanese War in a way that left neither with the upper hand. He also supported Hay's Open Door Policy in China because it encouraged a balance among all the major powers.

However much Hay tired of his Cassandra, he probably welcomed Adams's thoughts. The two agreed on the essentials if not on the gravity of the world situation. Adams served as a sounding board for Hay and generally reinforced his opinions, although Adams appeared to have no substantive influence on Hay's decisions.

Adams's friendship with Hay once again gave him an intimate view of government. But his privileged position did nothing to alter his growing determinism, and he continued to insist that circumstances dictated policy. Such an attitude seemed to contradict his own efforts on behalf of Cuba and his advice that the United States play a more active role in diplomacy. Here Adams confronted the problem of all determinists, from St. Augustine to his own Puritan fathers, but he did not tackle the dilemma head on. In musing on foreign or domestic concerns, he tended to act as if all were circumscribed by impersonal agents or by a fixed human nature. When it came to his own life, however, he acted as if he had free will. This contradiction permitted him to cope with existence. Nonetheless, there was a sense in which Adams could reconcile his bifurcated view of reality. He might claim, for instance, that an aggressive foreign policy resulted from prevailing conditions; it was irrelevant that governments assumed free will. Likewise, he could place his Cuban escapades within the context of economic, political, and cultural currents of which he was a part; his actions were merely a cog in the working out of Cuba's destiny.

Whatever his part in cosmic necessity, Adams was sure as the twentieth century began that the country had embarked on a new and unsettling course. The facts of geography, economy, and human nature had deprived the American people of their noble dream. They were destined for the common lot of humanity. They had lost their innocence and had come of age.

VII

Fin de Siècle and
the Revolt of Woman

LAMENTING his country's failures as well as his own and plagued with grief, Adams found refuge in foreign travel. In 1886 he spent several months in Japan with painter John La Farge and during the period 1890–1892, the two undertook an around-the-world voyage. From then on Adams passed seven or eight months of each year in Paris or its vicinity. He usually left Washington in May and did not return until the following January. Adams's travels gave him a wider perspective upon the ills of the modern world and helped him to relate his own nation's shortcomings to them. In particular, his jaunts introduced him to the idea of *fin de siècle* decadence and to the revolt of woman. Both phenomena deepened his belief that the cultures of the West, the American experiment included, were in decline.

Fin de siècle, meaning literally "end of the century," was a term applied by French critics to an atmosphere of social and cultural exhaustion that coincided with the waning years of the nineteenth century. Some pointed to the violence and immorality of realist and naturalist literature, while others disparaged the banality of impressionist painting or the senseless cacophony of contemporary music. An unnerving school of philosophy, headed by Henri Bergson, offered a strange mysticism. The old certainities and uniformities collapsed as avant-garde writers, artists, musicians, and thinkers attacked all that was stable or conventional.

Adams wandered into this confusion in the autumn of 1891 when he arrived in Paris on the last leg of his around-the-world tour. The mood of the city quite matched his own. He was desperately yet hopelessly in love. In his sorrow over Marian's death he had turned for solace to beautiful Elizabeth Cameron, one of Marian's closest friends. Since her husband Donald was very much alive, Adams's love was a constant source of frustration. During his recent voyage he had thought of her constantly and had written to her of all that he had seen and done. The two planned to meet in Paris, but their rendezvous went badly, each finding the situation awkward and strained. When she left for the United States a couple of weeks later, Henry was depressed and fled to England and his old friend Charles Milnes Gaskell. There he poured out his heart to Elizabeth whom he imagined was steaming along the Irish coast: "I have passed a bad *quart d'heure* since bidding you good-bye. . . . You saw and said that my Paris experiment was not so successful as you had meant it to be. Perhaps I should have done better not to have tried it."

In December he was back in Paris, blaming himself for the failure of their reunion and face to face with his anguish. While there he read a sampling of modern French fiction, a pastime punctuated with visits to the opera and theater. At the Opéra Comique he heard Richard Gentry's *Richard Coeur de Lion,* an opera that John Quincy Adams had attended a hundred years earlier. The grandson remembered being told how the old man, after his defeat in the presidential race of 1828, had associated himself with Richard. He paced the floor and muttered over and over again, *"Oh Richard, Oh mon roi. L'univers t'abandonne."*

Like his ancestor, Adams had a taste for melodrama and he wallowed in self-pity. He had lost his wife only to fall in love with a woman he could not have. And at age fifty-three, in spite of successful careers as journalist, professor, and historian, he insisted that he had fallen short of the family's standard of accomplishment.

Adams continued to write to Elizabeth often in letters that described the decadence of France and of Europe in general. He did not paint a comprehensive portrait of the *fin de siècle* landscape, and he was prone to exaggerate what he saw. He seemed to revel in accounts of decay. In fact, Adams affected a decadent pose, insisting that he and everything else in the world were going to hell together.

One missive to Elizabeth conveyed his mood of lively disgust with contemporary French novels: "Imagine my state of happiness, surrounded by a pile of yellow literature, skimming a volume of Goncourt, swallowing a volume of Maupassant with my roast, and wondering that I feel unwell afterwards." His reactions to Emile Zola were much the same. Zola had tried to render life as it really was and had had a propensity to dwell upon the baser side of human behavior. Men and women were not much better than beasts, possessing only a thin veneer of restraint. Zola chronicled the selfishness of the bourgeois investor, the unashamed sensuality of the prostitute and the lesbian, the viciousness of the hard-pressed peasant, the depravity of the slum dweller, and the soullessness of the alcoholic. An uncompromising determinist, Zola insisted that his characters were the hapless victims of human nature and the environment, an analysis of the individual and society similar to Adams's.

Adams had little to say about French art, music, or philosophy. Politics were another matter. The French state was as sick as the nation's literature, the most shocking indication being the Dreyfus affair. If Adams had little sympathy for Jewish Captain Dreyfus, falsely accused of selling mili-

tary secrets to Germany, he despaired over the way authorities had bungled the matter. The army had shown incompetence in not catching the real traitor in the first place and
then had disgraced itself by covering its mistakes with forged
documents and perjury. The government had cooperated
in the conspiracy to suppress evidence, and Dreyfus's bla-
tantly unfair trials had exposed French jurisprudence to
the ridicule and mockery of the entire world. All were in-
dications of France's inability to keep its house in order
and of its general decline. To Hay he remarked, "The
Dreyfus business reflects the whole social, economical and
political condition of the country, — the hopeless collapse
of the machine."

France's problems were manifestations of a condition
plaguing all Europe. Decadent literature, international ten-
sions, and financial woes betokened a widespread deteri-
oration. "Here in France, and I think everywhere on the
Continent," Adams observed to Gaskell, "the old tone of
optimism, or even of resistance, has disappeared. Everyone —
absolutely everyone — so far as the press, or the arts, or political expressions go — seems agreed that the end is near. . . .
The decline of France is obvious, but France merely leads.
Decline is everywhere." Europe's troubles and those of the
United States were intertwined. Problems in both were "in
our system itself, and at the bottom of all modern society.
If we are diseased, so is all the world."

Zola had pointed out one of the more alarming particu-
lars of modern society, the equality of men and women in
their baseness. The view that women were no better than
men was repulsive to Adams, who saw women as guardians
of morality and as sources of comfort and understanding.
If Zola were correct, society along with the individual stood
to suffer greatly.

Adams considered the feminist movement of the late
nineteenth and early twentieth centuries to be a milder ex-
pression of what Zola had described in his books but an

event just as serious in the long run. Equal rights meant that women could enter the world outside the home, allowing them to become as debased as the modern male. But for women in the movement, equality represented the culmination of a struggle that had had its American roots in the reform ferment of the 1830s and 1840s. At the time of the pivotal Seneca Falls Convention of 1848, women had few legal rights. They could not sit on juries, sue or be sued, or enter into contracts. They were unable to dispose of their property without their husband's consent and, regardless of marital predicament, divorce was extremely difficult. There was no question of voting. And with the exceptions of Oberlin and Mount Holyoke, higher education was closed to to them. Under the leadership of individuals like Lucy Stone, Susan B. Anthony, and Elizabeth Cady Stanton, women began to seek an end to their legal inferiority. By the 1890s they had wrested from most states the right to sue, to enter contracts, and to control their property. Several western states had given them the right to vote, and they had access to many more colleges and universities. Nationwide suffrage still eluded them, and awesome legal and occupational hurdles remained. Even so, the feminist movement was well under way and could claim some significant victories.

Adams was hostile to the movement. The increasing number of women who were joining their "brothers" at work agitated him most of all. In rural America women had engaged in productive labor, often toiling beside their husbands in the fields, but with industrialization they entered the factories. Women also invaded clerical, secretarial, and sales positions. A handful of intelligent and ambitious women attempted to penetrate medicine and law. There "were myriads of new [female] types ... — telephone and telegraph-girls, shop-clerks, factory-hands." The census of 1890 revealed approximately 3.7 million women in the labor market. Nearly all, however, were single, widowed, or divorced, and the majority of these, perhaps three-fourths, were single and under twenty-five. At most four percent of married women were in the work force.

Whether or not Adams knew that most wives were not seeking gainful employment, he deplored the idea of working women in general. Working women could not function as good wives and mothers, and most middle- and upper-class Americans shared his attitude. Nature had made women more moral than men and therefore unfit for business, industry, and the professions. And the very characteristics that rendered women unfit for the marketplace qualified them for the more crucial task of safeguarding morality. It was their duty to compensate for the evil tendencies of the male. In the modern, industrial world, with its great material temptations, it was even more important for women to remain at home and uncorrupted; only then could they temper male avarice with gentleness and altruism. The home was supposed to be a sanctuary to which the harried husband might return for comfort, but women hardened by jobs could hardly perform their role of support effectively. Their "axis of rotation [always] had been the cradle and the family," Adams declared; any straying from this axis "and the family must pay for it." Society would bear the consequences, its foundations irreparably undermined. The American experiment could not stand the demise of the traditional household and its moral teaching.

The kinds of women Adams knew personally were not likely to work in a factory or department store. Yet he noticed that some women of his class — those with intelligence and education — wanted more than a domestic existence. His wife had been bright and well taught, and he might have suspected that her lack of intellectual outlet contributed to her suicide. Nevertheless, he insisted that intellectual assertiveness in women would bring them and society much unhappiness.

In *Democracy* and in his second novel *Esther* (1884),

Adams dealt with the plight of two young women unable to accept their assigned places. *Democracy's* Madeleine Lee flees from femininity from the outset of the book. In her bitterness and sorrow at the deaths of her husband and son, she seeks an escape from domestic life; she wishes to see if "the family [is] all that life [has] to offer." Once in Washington she displays masculine characteristics: She has a probing, analytical mind, is interested in politics, and is aggressive in her attempts to befriend congressmen and senators. Then she meets Senator Ratcliffe, who appeals to her "female nature." Ratcliffe insists that she marry him because his life lacks a gentle touch. More moral than he, she can help him to walk through the quicksands of politics. She almost responds to his pleas, unable to deny her nature altogether and attracted to the role of comforter and preceptor. She asks herself, "Was not his career a thousand times more important than hers? If he, in his isolation and his cares, needed her assistance, had she an excuse for refusing it?" Was her life so "precious that she could not afford to fling it into the gutter, if need be, on the bare chance of enriching some fuller existence?" In the end she denies her protective, maternal instincts and is completely miserable for it.

Esther Dudley lands in much the same situation in Adam's second novel. She falls in love with an Episcopalian clergyman named Stephen Hazard. When he asks for her hand, she refuses because she cannot share his convictions; her assertive intellect will not allow her the faith most women have. After Esther has firmly refused him, Hazard makes a final and desperate attempt to win her by appeals to her female nature, to her innate need to be wife and mother: "Can you, without feeling . . . , think of a future existence where you will not meet once more father or mother, husband or children? Surely the natural instincts of your sex must save you from such a creed!" An inner voice urges her, "Mistress, know yourself! Down on your knees, and

thank heaven fasting for a good man's love!" But like
Madeleine, she refuses to relent and must endure the sad
consequences.

The greatest difficulty for Madeleine, Esther, and many
real women was an inability to accept their proper roles,
and for this society had to shoulder some of the blame. Although Adams agreed with his era's glorification of wife
and mother, he objected to its squeamishness about sexual
reproduction. Society must extoll childbearing and make
women more willing to accept nature's dictates. Most ages
and peoples *had* praised women for their fecundity; they
had not been forced to suffer the pains of Victorian prudery.

One manifestation of the high regard for maternity in
ancient societies had been the worship of female deities, a
subject that engaged Adams as early as 1876 when he gave
a lecture to the Lowell Institute entitled "The Primitive
Rights of Women." In all primitive societies men had associated fruit-bearing earth with the womb and worshipped
both in the personages of Venus, Diana, Isis, Ceres, and
others. Adams and La Farge, during their circumnavigation
of the globe, had been enthralled with an ancient fertility
dance performed by Samoan natives. Puritanical western
missionaries had banned the dance, but the two Americans
delighted in encouraging its performance. A letter to Elizabeth Cameron described an especially skillful dancer: "Imagine the best female figure you ever saw, on about a six foot
scale, neck, breast, back, arms and legs, all absolutely Greek
in modeling and action, with such freedom of muscle and
motion as the Greeks themselves hardly knew."

But what most convinced Adams of society's desire to
revere women were his travels through France. After 1895
he made scores of visits to the celebrated French cathedrals
of the late Middle Ages, virtually all built in the twelfth
and thirteenth centuries and dedicated to the Virgin Mary.
All were Notre Dames, that at Paris being only the most
famous to foreigners. Anthropologists of Adams's day already

had associated the Virgin with ancient fertility goddesses, and the Catholic church for centuries had held her up as the essence of maternity. The Judeo-Christian tradition may have banished female deities; in the eyes of the laity she often was more important than Christ himself. To Adams this was evidence of an irrepressible craving to worship reproduction and motherhood. He treated this theme in several letters, in several chapters of the *Education*, and in his *Mont-Saint-Michel and Chartres* (1905). The last named, styled as an elaborate guidebook to two of France's magnificent works of religious architecture, contained Adams's most eloquent words on the subject of women and their place in the world.

Chartres was the Virgin's most renowned French shrine. The original cathedral had been built to house the tunic Mary supposedly had worn at the time of conception. To the inhibitants of Chartres she symbolized fecundity, and they prayed to this holiest of mothers to grant them children. Her fame spread far and wide, suppliants coming on foot hundreds of miles to implore her aid. Each year Henri III of France and his wife Louise of Austria walked barefoot from Paris in hopes that she would fructify their barren union. The royal couple and tens of thousands of humbler souls who looked to the Virgin were acting out a fertility rite not unlike that Adams and La Farge had witnessed in Samoa. The form was utterly different, the goal the same.

The Virgin also personified the forgiving, compassionate mother, she who was Mother of God. Sinners were confident that she understood their frailties, for she had been mortal herself. If her Son judged them too harshly, they knew that she would intercede to temper his wrath, just as their own mothers had intervened to quiet the anger of fathers or brothers.

Recognition of this overpowering love for the Virgin was necessary for a full appreciation of Chartres Cathedral. In their devotion to Mary the townspeople had wanted to erect the most splendid palace on earth. Men of all stations, from peasants to noble lords, had harnessed themselves like cattle to wagons in which they carted huge granite blocks from quarry to building site. Adams wrote that they looked upon the cathedral as a giant doll's house "to please the Queen of Heaven . . . — to charm her till she smiled."

Out of such faith and love had arisen one of the most beautiful works of art known to humanity. But this was not all that such faith had engendered; the cult of the Virgin had exerted a civilizing influence upon European society. Men and women were inspired to perform good deeds in her name, and even the rudest knights placed themselves at her service. Adams associated knightly devotion to Mary with the larger cult of medieval chivalry. High-born women of the period attempted to raise the moral tone of life. "They used every terror they could invent, as well as every tenderness they could invoke, to tame the beasts around them. Their charge was of manners, and, to teach manners, they made a school which they called their Court of Love." Adams attributed to medieval gentlewomen the same crucial function that he expected modern American women to perform, the promotion of moral well-being.

In *Chartres*, in his two novels, and elsewhere, Adams made clear his view of women's proper role. They were responsible for the moral education of their children and for the guidance of husbands, brothers, and fathers. They also had the duty of providing a sanctuary where the troubled male, bearing the scars of worldly strife, might find tenderness and compassion. For thousands of years society had venerated women for undertaking these charges. Unless modern women could emulate the Virgin of Chartres, the nation and the entire West would feel the sting of their failure. He himself, since Marian's death, had looked to women for sympathy and understanding. From Elizabeth Cameron, Mrs. Henry Cabot Lodge (whom he called Sister Anne), and several of his nieces, he expected pampering and maternal affection. To a female friend he wrote, "Women are naturally neither daughters, sisters, lovers, nor wives, but mothers."

Adams had strong misgivings about the women's rights movement. But *Democracy* and *Esther* betrayed his awareness that many intelligent, creative women could not find meaning and purpose in following the conventional route. Nevertheless, he believed that they had no choice but to accept their fate; he could not understand that women, like men, wanted to fulfill their human potential and to enjoy the American rights of liberty and happiness. Nor was Adams able to see that modern realistic literature was part of an exciting cultural flowering. Yet jaundiced though Adams was in his opinions of literature and the women's movement, he saw them in the perspective of a larger theme in modern life. In the next two decades he would fit these pieces into a wider panorama, fashioning from them a more comprehensive picture of decline.

VIII
Devolution

EVERYWHERE HE LOOKED Adams saw signs of social and cultural devolution. Yet he had not been able to integrate these into any grand theory to explain the parallel decay of America and Europe. Eventually, he found an answer in the continuing conflict between science and religion. The chaos of modern science was replacing the unity and purpose traditionally provided by religion.

Religion had given people a sense of order and meaning. Even when the great thinkers of post-Renaissance Europe discarded a wholly theological explanation of the universe, they did not initially deny that it was orderly and purposeful; in place of God's plan they substituted natural law. But by the end of the nineteenth century, Adams realized, many scientists and philosophers questioned the existence of natural law and with it all cosmic direction. Such skepticism was a serious blow to the American experiment, grounded as it was in eternal truths. Adams also believed that abandonment of natural law was at the heart of a general decline in Western civilization.

There was nothing new about the conflict between science and religion. It had been raging since the scientific revolution began in the sixteenth century, manifesting itself in

battles like that between Galileo and the Catholic church.
In the latter third of the nineteenth century it focused on
biological evolution. When Darwinists claimed that life had
evolved gradually over millions of years, religious funda-
mentalists decried their theories as an attack upon the
Genesis story of creation. Even more open-minded Christians were shaken by the suggestion that a purely physical
struggle to survive had transformed species. Such a doctrine
represented the grossest philosophical materialism and
seemed to undermine the need for a supernatural agency.
In time most liberal Christians were able to embrace evolution by proposing that scientists still could not explain how
the primal matter of the universe was created and how it was
infused with life. Nor could scientists disprove that the hand
of God had ordained the laws of evolution as part of his
divine plan.

Adams dealt with the compromise between liberal Christianity and evolution in *Esther*. Esther's Reverend Hazard
believes he has resolved the conflict between science and
religion. In the very first sermon she hears him preach, he
declares that there can be no war between the two, for
everything in the universe, including the scientific method
itself, is but an emanation of the divine mind. The minister
welcomes the scientist to "analyze, dissect, use [his] micro-
scope or [his] spectrum till the last atom of matter is
reached." No discovery can shake the church because the
faithful know that science "will find enthroned behind all
thought and matter" the supreme Creator and Sustainer of
the universe.

Esther, reared by an agnostic father, is not convinced,
and doubt makes her refuse Hazard in the end. She tries
with all her might to accept his beliefs, poring over volumes
of theology and plaguing everyone around her with endless
queries. She even turns to her cousin George Strong, a professional geologist and also an agnostic. In answer to her
demands to know if religion is true, he insists that it is a

matter of faith alone. Explaining that she cannot will herself faith, he responds that everybody believes in something:
"There is no science which does not begin by requiring you
to believe the incredible." Esther still finds it easier to
accept the rational and empirical proofs of science than to
take up religious propositions on the authority of faith.

Adams clearly shared Esther's anguish. He too was an
agnostic and craved the solace of religious faith, particularly
after Marian's death. In the prayer he wrote while working
on the *Chartres*, he addressed the Virgin, imploring her
understanding and faith:

> Help me to see! not with my mimic sight —
> With yours! which carried radiance, like the sun,
> Giving the rays you saw with — light in light —
> Tying all suns and stars and worlds in one.
>
> Help me to know! not with my mocking art —
> With you, who knew yourself unbound by laws;
> Gave God your strength, your life, your sight, your heart,
> And took from him the Thought that Is — the Cause.
>
> Help me to feel! not with my insect sense, —
> With yours that felt all life alive in you;
> Infinite heart beating at your expense;
> Infinite passion breathing the breath you drew!
>
> Help me to bear! not my own baby load,
> But yours; who bore the failure of the light,
> The strength, the knowledge and the thought of God, —
> The futile folly of the Infinite!

Adams wanted faith not only for himself; he believed it
essential for society as a whole. Otherwise there could be no
order and purpose. It need not be religious faith; natural
law would do almost as well. In *Mont-Saint-Michel and
Chartres*, however, he dwelt upon the role of medieval religion in providing society with unity and direction. This
atmosphere of order and purpose, Adams asserted, was best

reflected in ecclesiastical art and architecture. Taine, along with other nineteenth-century critics such as John Ruskin, Jacob Burckhardt, and Viollet-le-Duc, had proclaimed that art was one of the surest guides to understanding a historical epoch. Adams, who had read them all, applied their dictum to the churches of medieval France. *Mont-Saint-Michel and Chartres* focused upon two of the great works of medieval French architecture, the abbey church at Mont-Saint-Michel and the cathedral at Chartres. Both represented the oneness and purpose of medieval life, each in a different light.

The abbey church, perched atop a steep granite mount just off the Normandy coast, expressed the unity of the Church Militant, of the conquering eleventh-century Norman. Heavy rounded arches bespoke masculine strength, as did the figure of Saint Michael astride the central tower. Sword uplifted, he trampled a vanquished Satan. The warrior and the church were united; abbots, monks, kings, poets, and princes were all welcome at the abbey and were as likely to sing the deeds of valiant knights as to chant hymns of praise to the Lord. The abbey church on the mount "expressed the unity of Church and State, God and Man, Peace and War, Life and Death, Good and Bad; it solved the whole problem of the universe." Men of sword and cloth joined in the work of God: The knight went forth to conquer new lands for Christendom, while the priest blessed his work. Both pursued a purposeful existence.

Though impressed with the spirit of Mont-Saint-Michel, it was not the eleventh-century Church Militant that Adams most admired. Rather it was the Church Triumphant of the twelfth and thirteenth centuries, symbolized by Chartres Cathedral. By then the church's otherworldliness had triumphed over the martial spirit. At Chartres, begun about 1100, the Gothic vault had replaced the heavier, earthbound Romanesque. Thrusting into the heavens and pointing ever upward, Gothic forms tore people's hearts from the earthly and profane. The gentle, forgiving figure of the Virgin and not the warlike Saint Michael reigned here. She promised salvation to all who asked for it and her promise united all in hope. Caring little about strict theology, the worshippers at Chartres relegated Father, Son, and Holy Ghost to secondary positions and sought them only through the Virgin. The cathedral's iconography demonstrated clearly that Mary was supreme in the eyes of the faithful. She appeared in glass and stone more often than any other religious subject.

All Western Europe then joined in one faith and in the assurance that the Christian's purpose in this world was to obey God's moral law and to prepare for the afterlife. Such was far from the case in modern Europe or America. Instead of order and purpose there was moral and intellectual confusion, individuals and nations not knowing what they ultimately wanted or needed. Men might be intent on making vast sums of money or achieving national glory, but their goals had no grounding in absolutes. Rebellious women and decadent artists suffered from the same moral and intellectual confusion. From the unity of the twelfth century, civilization had moved to the disorder or multiplicity of the twentieth. And since Adams viewed this movement as negative and regressive, he asserted that Western society was undergoing devolution, a movement that explained the simultaneous decay of Europe and America.

Here Adams challenged the social evolutionists. Darwin, Spencer, and other evolutionists had shared a tendency to see all reality in terms of gradual, upward development, as opposed to the more static eighteenth-century view of the universe. Adams used Spencer's particular concept of evolution as a basis for his own theories of devolution. Spencer saw evolution as the inexorable movement from chaotic, undifferentiated homogeneity to ordered, differentiated het-

erogeneity. All the matter in the cosmos had begun as a
swirling mass of simple, uniform particles that had combined into larger and more varied forms performing complex functions. Primitive atoms and molecules had developed into stars, planets, rocks, trees, rabbits, and human
beings. The result was an ordered functioning of the material universe, each complex body behaving in a regular
and predictable way.

By analogy, Spencer applied the same process to human
society. Primitive groups were like the primordial universe.
Individuals in early societies were homogeneous in function,
and there were no elaborate institutions. Over time intricate
divisions of labor emerged, as did highly developed institutions, bringing with them more and more social order. Society thereby progressed from the simple, the undifferentiated, and the chaotic to the complex, the differentiated,
and the ordered. Spencer supposed, however, that there was
a limit. Society would reach a state wherein further complexity was impossible and counterproductive and would
then enter a stagnant phase or even start to degenerate.
Here was Adams's point of departure. Proposing that society
already had entered that period at which additional heterogeneity was impossible, he claimed that devolution had
begun.

Adams was content to borrow from Spencer the broad
concept of movement from simplicity and homogeneity to
complexity and heterogeneity. Instead of finding comparative disorder in all earlier stages of civilization, however,
Adams maintained that certain previous epochs had been
marked by much greater order than that in the present.
Undoubtedly he drew this conclusion because he believed
the West was already in decline.

Adams examined the causes of twentieth-century disorder
in the autobiographical *Education of Henry Adams* and in
two pamphlets addressed to the historical community. The
Education together with the *Chartres,* he asserted, were

attempts to trace the development of Western civilization from the High Middle Ages to the twentieth century. Referring to himself in the third person, he explained, "Eight or ten years of study had led Adams to think he might use the century 1150–1250 . . . as the unit from which he might measure motion down to his own time." In the *Chartres* he had elaborated that unit in great detail. From it "he proposed to fix a position for himself, which he could label: 'The Education of Henry Adams: A Study of Twentieth-Century Multiplicity.'" *Unity* and *multiplicity* became his terms for Spencer's *order* and *disorder*.

Actually the *Education* did not treat the decline of unity since the High Middle Ages. Adams confined his analysis and descriptions to his lifetime. Using himself as a measuring rod for the decline of unity in his own day, he opened the *Education* with the claims that he had begun life in an eighteenth-century world even though he was born in 1838. The Adamses continued to believe firmly in the essential unity and purpose of the cosmos and had passed this philosophy on to Henry. Such a world view was not only a holdover from the Enlightenment but was also a secular equivalent to the mind of the twelfth and thirteenth centuries.

In later life these familial beliefs proved to be handicaps. Adams lived in a time that rejected these beliefs, and he was ill equipped to adjust; neither parents or teachers had prepared him. He had tried to catch up with a rapidly changing world by starting his education all over again, serving as his own teacher. But whatever he learned was antiquated before he mastered it. The story of his life had been one futile attempt after another to obtain the right knowledge: hence the title *The Education of Henry Adams.*

Adams concluded that his failure to learn was due to the rapidity with which scholars and researchers uncovered new information; his contemporaries, of course, lived under the same disadvantage. The twentieth century had ushered in a knowledge explosion. Too much information was revealed at too rapid a rate for anyone to make it part of the old unities let alone to come up with new syntheses. Intellectual chaos reigned in every area of human endeavor. As Adams colorfully described it, humanity had entered "a far vaster universe, where all the old roads ran about in every direction, overrunning, dividing, subdividing, stopping abruptly, vanishing slowly, with side-paths that led nowhere, and sequences that could not be proved."

But confusion was only one part of the tale. Adams learned, upon reading Karl Pearson's *Grammar of Science* and other works on the philosophy of science, that leading thinkers denied the existence of natural law altogether. Even if it were possible to keep abreast of new knowledge, there were no longer laws or unities around which to organize it. Order, law, unity, purpose, and the like were mere constructs of the mind, whose objective existence could not be verified. The honest scientist must be content with the facts of sensate experience and the apparent causal relations among them. He could not even prove that his facts and their connections existed objectively.

Pearson's admonitions reflected the pragmatic mood of the early twentieth century. Pragmatists such as William James and John Dewey proposed that a scientific theory or any sort of proposition was true if it worked, if it allowed the experimenter to account for a given situation. Propositions were not true, however, in an absolute sense; they were not eternal or cosmic law. Implicit in pragmatism was an assertion of free will; for both James and Dewey, life made little sense if it were determined by ironclad natural law. Pragmatism freed the individual to create truth as he or she operated in the world.

Adams, already a confirmed historical determinist, dismissed pragmatism at once. It contradicted his own conclusions and was highly dangerous besides, for people always had needed some absolute. Whether by asserting the reality of supernatural force or of natural law, individuals had looked at themselves in a unified, ordered, purposeful world. The new position deprived them of the only cosmic security they had known and made them aimless wanderers on an accidental and purposeless planet. It also played havoc with the life of nations, leaving them without a goal beyond mere survival. Certainly the American experiment had no chance at all if its mooring in natural law were completely destroyed. Good government would prove impossible without moral guides: States would operate on grounds of expediency alone. Without its "laws of Nature and Nature's God," the United States was lost. Under the circumstances Adams had "a vehement wish to escape." He longed for "his eighteenth-century education when God was a father and nature a mother, and all was for the best in a scientific universe."

The world had traveled a long way since the childhood of Henry Adams, and even further since the people of Chartres had erected their monument of love to the Virgin Queen, their symbol of a "unified universe." The electrical dynamo was now the ruling deity, and Adams found it a fitting symbol for the multiplicity of the twentieth century. The device first captured his attention at the Columbian Exposition of 1893 and continued to fascinate him at the Paris Exposition of 1900 and the St. Louis World's Fair of 1904. To these gigantic engines modern citizens dedicated their genius and money, as society eight hundred years earlier had lavished its intelligence and wealth on cathedrals. But the dynamo did not unify the world as had the Virgin. Rather, it created confusion as it drove machinery and altered life in ways that none understood and that none were prepared to handle.

The devolution from Virgin to dynamo was tragic but inevitable, dictated by the inescapable laws of history. Adams described these forces in one of the final chapters of the *Education* entitled "A Dynamic Theory of History." He began by declaring the supreme importance of thought in all human action and ultimately in all forms of civilization. History was the record of thought. The motor of history was a dialectic between mind and nature, each acting upon the other. In humanity's infancy their mutual attraction had been weak, but as nature exposed itself to mind and as mind acquired more ways of probing nature, their interaction grew more forceful and rapid, resembling two celestial bodies moving toward each other. Indeed, Adams made a direct comparison between the dialectic of mind and nature and a comet's elongated orbit around the sun. At aphelion, the point in orbit furthest from the sun, the comet moved slowly — not unlike the primitive mind. Moving closer to the sun, it accelerated until, rounding the sun, it began its decelerating journey toward aphelion once again. If the analogy were correct, it followed that there would be a limit to intellectual acceleration, at which point mind would collapse into hopeless chaos and begin to regress.

The dynamic theory of history resembled his brother Brooks's law of civilization and decay. Brooks held that people's desire for power had passed through religious, military, and commercial stages. Henry simplified by making the search for power wholly intellectual. Both theories proposed limits to the acquisition of power. Brooks asserted that too great a concentration would end in social collapse; Henry maintained that too much knowledge, which in turn produced power, would lead to the devolution of Western civilization. Both Adamses looked for the motive force of history in human nature, Brooks in fear and Henry in curiosity.

Dissatisfied with his dynamic theory, Adams addressed two pamphlets to fellow historians, "The Rule of Phase Applied to History" (1909) and "A Letter to American Teachers of History" (1910). With the aid of J. Franklin Jameson, managing editor of the *American Historical Review*, he sent copies to professional historians throughout the United States. The earlier piece drew an analogy between stages of social development and the rule of phase, a theory propounded by Yale physicist Josiah Willard Gibbs. The rule involved a set of mathematical formulas that determined the point at which heterogeneous substances were in equilibrium — as, for example, the coexistence of ice and water in a closed system. Gibbs calculated how much heat energy, added or subtracted, upset their equilibrium. Factors of pressure and volume also influenced equilibrium, and Gibbs was able to calculate these too.

From Gibbs's theory Adams proposed that a disruption in the balance of heterogeneous substances was similar to the passage of societies from one historical phase to another. Various states of mind coexisted in all societies, but one always predominated and gave life its overall complexion. This prevailing spirit held sway until some force disrupted the mental equilibrium. In his analogy with the rule of phase Adams substituted the terms *attraction* for *pressure* and *acceleration* for *temperature,* but he kept the word *volume.* By attraction he meant the forces that mind and nature exerted on each other. Acceleration was the increasing rate at which the two factors interacted, while volume referred to the size and scope of the society in question.

Borrowing from Comte once more, Adams declared that Western civilization had passed through two major equilibriums and was about to enter a third and fourth, each associated with the prevailing type of thought. The religious phase had lasted until about 1600 when Bacon, Descartes, and others introduced secular scientific thought. The most important personality of the age was Isaac Newton, who had constructed a mechanistic view of the universe and had opened a second, mechanical phase. Newton's scheme had dominated until recently, being superseded by the new electromagnetic synthesis. The dynamo presided over what Adams called the electrical phase, an epoch beginning about 1900.

Adams now wished to calculate how long the current phase would last. Returning to his comet analogy, he suggested that the interaction between mind and nature accelerated according to the law of squares. He then took the square root of 300, the length of the mechanical era (1600–1900), and came up with seventeen and a half years for the electrical phase. If the law held true, society would enter yet another stage lasting about four years, the approximate square root of 17. He named it the ethereal phase, believing that ether was the physicochemical state beyond electricity. At this juncture further equilibriums would be impossible, thought having reached its limits. Either intellectual stagnation or chaos would result. Accordingly, the end would come about 1921, at the close of the brief ethereal epoch.

Adams's second pamphlet, "A Letter to American Teachers of History," attempted to forge another analogy between history and the physical sciences, this time with the second law of thermodynamics, or the law of entropy. The second law stated that the process of releasing heat energy always resulted in its degradation. Adams equated heat energy with social energy, a term he did not define. Social energy, governed by the second law, would come to the same end as physical energy in the solar system, flowing to ever lower levels until it could do no more work. It would be as if all the sun's energy had passed over a waterfall into a vast and stagnant pool; eventually the sun would consume all its fuel and burn itself out. On earth people assisted in the degradation of the solar system's supply of energy. "Man dissipates every year," Adams wrote, "all the heat stored in a thousand million tons of coal which nature herself cannot now replace." In doing so he transformed "some ten or fifteen per cent of it into mechanical energy immediately wasted on his transient and commonly purposeless objects." Society, too, was bound to degenerate as its energies descended from one irretrievable level to the next. Rather than evolving, as Social Darwinists claimed, Western civilization was devolving. At last Adams had found a theory that completely overturned Darwinism, about which he had had misgivings for some time.

Adams's analogies strained the reader's credulity, but Adams himself saw them as half fanciful excursions into model building. When several who had received pamphlets took them too seriously, he complained to Brooks, "The fools begin at once to discuss whether the theory was true." Surely social energy could not be equated with heat energy, or the development of thought with a comet's orbit, and Adams was the first to admit it. His analogies were merely aids to comprehension. The historian needed "technical tools quite as much as the electrician does; large formulas . . . [and] generalizations, no matter how temporary or hypothetical." But if Adams was not adamant about his particular models of devolution, he was certain that the American experiment was in great peril. It was hopelessly enmeshed in forces dragging all Western civilization toward decay and death.

IX
Futility

Adams's flight into esoteric theories of history by no means indicated that he had lost interest in politics. As the progressive reformers gained strength in the federal government, his critical powers were aroused, and he unleashed a stream of abuse against the new reformers and their designs. He was no less hard on himself, insisting that his life had been as futile as the progressive program. If he and his generation had failed to save the American experiment, at least he took comfort in knowing that the present group of reformers would fare no better in the face of inescapable devolution.

The assassination of President McKinley in 1901 immediately focused Adams's attention upon politics, for it swept his friend Theodore Roosevelt into office. Adams had befriended Roosevelt through their mutual association with Henry Cabot Lodge. During the years that TR was in Washington as civil service commissioner (1889–1895), Adams had entertained him frequently; now his Theodore was a fellow resident of Lafayette Square.

From the outset Roosevelt's behavior in the White House fascinated Adams. TR was the first president since Lincoln to use the full potential of his office and frequently did so in a colorful and belligerent manner. To Adams he seemed like a pampered young bull intent on getting his own way. His amusement soon mixed with disgust as Roosevelt showed increasing sympathy with the progressive cause.

A host of difficulties accompanying rapid industrialization could no longer be ignored. Muckraking journalists had aroused the anger and concern of many citizens; cheap mass-circulation newspapers and magazines gave them a much wider audience than Adams had enjoyed a generation earlier. Waste and inefficiency in government disgusted engineers and managers. Small businessmen feared competition from larger and more productive enterprises, and middle-class consumers blamed rising prices on monopolies. Finally, many members of the middle class envisioned a proletarian uprising if employers did not treat workers more equitably. The continuing discontent of farmers and industrial workers added strength to the progressive movement, although the two groups often were at odds over issues and did not always see eye to eye with the middle-class reformers who dominated it.

Convinced that any reform would be fruitless, Adams charged that Roosevelt courted progressives solely to advance his political fortunes. The president's attacks on big business were largely verbal and unsystematic. Equally suspicious was Roosevelt's distinction between "good and bad trusts." In Adams's opinion giant combinations were an integral part of modern life and no one, not even the president of the United States with the full cooperation of Congress and the courts, could actually limit their power. Full-scale war on the trusts would only weaken the economy and hasten the day of judgment. To Brooks he announced, "The whole fabric of our society will go to wreck if we really lay hands of reform on our rotten institutions." Whatever Roosevelt and the reformers did, the result would be the same — collapse. As in 1896 the idea of a sudden catastrophe sometimes excited Adams; and in such moods he hailed antitrust suits as the surest means to quick disaster. On other occasions he denounced the trustbusters, wishing that the day of reckoning might be postponed until he had passed from the scene. Such sentiments were expressed partly tongue in cheek; nevertheless, he was sure that Roosevelt and the reformers were wasting their time.

Adams was just as contemptuous of Roosevelt's successor William Howard Taft. He had liked Taft in the beginning, but before long he came to see the president's huge size and lethargic demeanor as symbolic of his whole administration. "The longer I live under this Cincinnati régime," he complained to Elizabeth Cameron, "the cheaper and commoner and fatter I find it." Taft's vigorous enforcement of the Sherman Act was as pointless as Roosevelt's. When 1912 rolled around, he characterized the three-cornered race among Roosevelt, Taft, and Woodrow Wilson as a farce and refused to take seriously either the New Nationalism or the New Freedom. All three were tilting at windmills. He wished the victor well, but he was confident that Wilson's reform program would fail to cure the country's terminal illnesses. One afternoon during the Wilson administration he turned to young Assistant Secretary of the Navy Franklin Roosevelt, whom he had invited to tea, and said, "I've watched people come into the White House and I've watched them go from the White House. Really what they do there doesn't matter a great deal."

Resigned to the country's decay, Adams began calling himself a Conservative Christian Anarchist. Like a Christian of the late Roman Empire, he felt helpless to arrest the decline, and at the same time he looked forward to seeing the old, decadent order take its place in the trash heap of worn-out civilizations. He only wished the end might come without too much pain. Fond of imagining himself one of the church fathers living in the twilight of the ancient world, he wrote to Brooks, "I can always find amusement in reading Symmachus and St. Augustine, but what can I do about it, — play Symmachus, or play St. Augustine?" Un-like them he had no faith to sustain him or to offer hope for the future: "Exactly and literally, I find myself in the very skin of St. Jerome, but without Scriptures to vulgarize."

If Adams was hard on the new breed of reformers, he was equally hard on himself. In the *Education* he bemoaned his inadequacies at every step. Always he had fallen short of his own and society's expectations and had remained pain-fully ignorant in an ever-changing world. On graduating from Harvard, "he knew nothing. Education had not be-gun." After spending the next two years in Europe he knew no more. The seven years in London as private secretary were equally barren. Returning to Harvard after two worth-less years as a reform journalist, he had tried not to repeat the mistakes of his teachers, but was as ineffective as they. Then having chronicled the disasters of his youth, he barely mentioned the next two decades of life, including the hap-piest and most productive of all. And so the *Education* continued until his final despair at the acceleration of knowledge and the larger collapse of Western civilization.

As friends and associates died, Adams included them in the litany of failure. After reading Henry James's biography of fellow Bostonian William Wetmore Story, he wrote to James that their own and Story's generation were of "one mind and nature." They had been prepared to take active roles in public life, but the citizenry had rejected them. Their educations had paid few appreciable dividends.

When George Cabot Lodge, son of Henry Cabot Lodge, died suddenly at age thirty-six, Adams added him to the roll of futile lives. He was fond of Lodge and had spent much time with him in Paris, where the young man had gone to study literature and write poetry. Lodge became a fellow Conservative Christian Anarchist and often turned to Adams for avuncular advice, asking him to criticize his verse. In a short memorial biography, *The Life of George Cabot Lodge* (1911), Adams depicted young Lodge as another victim of New England society. Like Adams, Lodge had hated the bankers of Boston's State Street and much preferred the family's summer house in Nahant to its residence in the city. Lodge's career in literature was doomed from the start because practical, materialistic New Englanders had little taste for deep feeling, nor did most Americans of the late nineteenth and early twentieth centuries. Lodge had even failed to evoke controversy over his poetry; his verse fell into a sea of indifference. The poet's lines had met the same dead end, Adams thought, as had his own in the *History*.

John Hay's death presented Adams with a wholly different situation. When Clara Hay asked Adams to edit her husband's letters and to write a short introduction to them, he knew he could not represent his friend's life as one of futility. Hay had died at the height of success just as negotiations with the Russians and Japanese bore fruit and just as his long efforts at rapprochement between the United States and Great Britain were beginning to mature. These were but culminations of a constantly active, practical life. He had craved a diplomatic career as early as the 1860s and had bided his time, playing the game of politics and working at a variety of jobs until McKinley and Roosevelt gave him the opportunity to act on a broad stage.

Adams could not have missed the parallels between Hay and Gallatin. Both had used their extraordinary talents to serve the public as events permitted; they had acted in the best Adams tradition. Privately Adams might answer that Hay had been a mere tool of political and economic necessity. Even so, Hay's life and accomplishments must have made Adams uncomfortable about his own reluctance to employ his talents where he could, compromising when required, refusing to give up, and waiting until his chance came. Hay along with Roosevelt had proved that intelligent gentlemen could make a mark in public life. They did not solve all the problems of their day, but they did deal successfully with several foreign and domestic difficulties and

paved the way for future successes. Adams's failure was
partly his own making, and in his more honest moments he
must have known it.

The pessimism and self-castigation of the *Education* and
other mature writings obscured a very warm and affable
side to Adams's life. In his later years he retained many
friends from the past and continued to make new ones. And
nobody could be more solicitous of those for whom he cared.
His humor was also unimpaired, particularly at the expense
of public figures. He wrote to Elizabeth that he frequently
saw President Wilson strolling by his window with his
fiancée Mrs. Gault. "You've no idea," he quipped, "how
sweet it is when they kiss each other out walking." His love
of theater, opera, and fine restaurants was as strong as ever,
and he could enjoy such activities now on an income of
around $60,000 annually.

Another source of satisfaction for the aging Adams was
the enthusiastic reception of the *Education* and the *Chartres*, both of which he had had printed privately, distrib-
uting several hundred copies to those he thought would
appreciate them properly. Almost immediately he received
scores of requests from others. Commercial publishers began
plaguing him, too, for permission to reprint. Adams finally
allowed the American Institute of Architects to put out an
edition of the *Chartres*, and it met with great applause
when it was released in November 1913. He steadfastly refused to publish the *Education* during his own lifetime, but
he gave the Massachusetts Historical Society authority to
issue it posthumously.

By now Adams was balder than ever and only a fringe of
grey hair decorated the sides and back of his head, while a
full beard and mustache masked the entire lower part of the
face. He was also plumper yet by no means fat. His health
was declining a bit; an eye condition diagnosed as iritis
made it increasingly difficult for him to read during the
day or to venture outside until evening. In July 1908 he

suffered a slight stroke, but he was relatively sound until laid low by several severe seizures in April 1912.

Adams was cognizant of how closely he had brushed death. In several letters he made a pretense of anger at having been cheated out of his grave, but in truth he was happy to be alive and went on to enjoy the next six years as he had no other time in his life, save the dozen years with Marian. No one expected much of him now and it was too late to make a great mark on the world. He returned to his habit of spending seven or eight months of the year abroad and was in France when war broke out in August 1914. For him the conflict was undeniable proof that the collapse of civilization as he knew it was near at hand. And in a way he was correct. Although the certainties of the nineteenth century had been under attack for several decades, it took World War I to shatter society's faith in automatic progress and natural law. In spite of his excessive pessimism and his tortured scientific analogies, he was right in believing that his world would not last beyond the terminal date 1921.

In his mellower moods, Adams did not rail against fate, and he even took satisfaction in his country's intervention on behalf of Britain and France. His Atlantic alliance was a reality, and as in 1898, he was proud of America's new weight in international affairs. He looked forward to one day at a time, happy to have another reprieve.

On the morning of March 27, 1918, when Adams did not come downstairs at the usual hour, a niece and one of her friends went up to his room and found him dead, lying on his bed, but fully dressed for the day's activities. On the twenty-eighth the rector of nearby St. John's Episcopal Church read a simple service in the house, and then Adams's remains were taken to Rock Creek Cemetery, where he joined Clover at last.

It is possible that Adams died hoping against hope that the American experiment might succeed in spite of what had befallen it. On the last page of the *Education* he had

imagined a return to earth with Hay and King on their cen-
tenaries: "Perhaps, then, for the first time since man began
his education among the carnivores, they would find a world
that sensitive and timid natures could regard without a
shudder."

But mostly he doubted that the world of 1938 would be
an improvement over his own. He offered no final summary
of his doubts, yet his conclusions were clear. There was the
matter of human nature: The American people were no
better and no worse than their European forebears and
therefore incapable of building a better society. In this
regard Adams was much more pessimistic than his great-
grandfather and others in the family who had believed that
perseverance by the wise and virtuous might improve humanity's lot, if only in small measure. Henry's refusal to
admit the possibility of progress resulted partly from temperament but also from far-reaching changes in American
life that made it more difficult for him to participate in
government than his ancestors.

Both Jacksonian Democracy and the industrial revolution altered the conditions and rules under which the
national experiment had been launched. Egalitarianism virtually demolished the older eighteenth-century habit of
deference to social and intellectual betters. Industrialization with its concomitant growth of population and cities
also mitigated against deference, making it more difficult
for the voter to single out the natural aristocrat. As con-
stituencies became larger and as geographical mobility increased, the former intimacy among neighbors of differing
ability and social standing declined, leaving the voter open
to manipulation by anonymous political machines.

Finally, there was confusion during the late nineteenth
and early twentieth centuries over the country's goals. What
originally had been an endeavor to raise the American
people morally, intellectually, and materially had turned
into a race for economic success. The advent of pragmatism

and the accompanying decline of moral and intellectual absolutes were especially worrisome to Adams. If he could have chosen any words to express this concern, he might have selected them from a letter he wrote to J. Franklin Jameson in November 1910. He was musing over the meaning of the last half century and was more than ever struck by the atmosphere of confusion and uncertainty that had enveloped the nation since the beginning of the Civil War. More than anything else it was this lack of direction that would administer the final blow: "Fifty years ago last month, I went back to America to vote for honest Abe Lincoln and today I ought to be there to vote for somebody, but the fifty years of experience leave me quite in the dark. . . . Yet I have almost recovered . . . by realising that the world seems actually as much in the dark as I, and realises, as I do, that it suffers from senile decay. . . . Last winter I thought I ought not to publish the pessimism of Europe, and so risk perverting the childlike innocence of America, but . . . [the] American world has no longer any virginity to lose. . . . Fifty years ago we fought, — God knows why, — but we believed in it. Whom ought I to fight now?"

A Note on the Sources

ADAMS WAS a prolific writer. Nearly all his extant correspondence is at the Massachusetts Historical Society and the Houghton Library, Harvard University, and is available on microfilm to scholars. A number of letters have been published. *A Cycle of Adams Letters, 1861–1865,* edited by Worthington C. Ford (2 vols., Boston, 1920), contains selections from Adams's wartime correspondence as well as letters by his father and brothers. More complete are *Letters of Henry Adams, 1858–1891* (Boston, 1930) and *Letters of Henry Adams, 1892–1918* (Boston, 1938), also edited by Worthington C. Ford. *Henry Adams and his Friends* (Boston, 1947), edited by Harold Dean Cater, contains letters concerning Adams's private life. Cater's lengthy introduction sheds additional light on Adams at home. *Letters to a Niece* (Boston, 1920) comprises his missives to Mabel Hooper La Farge and underlines the importance of Adams's nieces in his later life.

Adams published extensively and all his works are essential to an understanding of him. As a young man he wrote for the *Harvard Magazine* and was correspondent for several newspapers, including the Boston *Courier,* the Boston *Advertiser,* and the *New York Times.* While a free-lance journalist, he placed articles in the *Nation,* the *North American Review,* and several British periodicals. From the late 1870s to the early 1890s, he concentrated on history, turning out *The Life of Albert Gallatin* (Philadelphia, 1879), and *John Randolph* (Boston, 1882), along with a nine-volume *History of the United States of America during the Administrations of Thomas Jefferson and James Madison* (New York, 1889–1891). He also wrote two novels, *Democracy* (New York, 1880) and *Esther* (New York, 1884). At the turn of the century he produced his travel books, *Tahiti* (1901) and *Mont-Saint-*

Michel and Chartres (1905), both privately printed. In the next several years he returned to history, composing two essays on the science of history: "The Rule of Phase Applied to History" (1909) and "A Letter to American Teachers of History" (1910). Then there was his so-called autobiography, *The Education of Henry Adams* (Boston, 1918). The work contains much information unavailable elsewhere, but one must be wary of Adams's distortions and self-depreciations. Rounding out his writings were his introduction to the *Letters of John Hay* (Washington, D.C., 1908) and *The Life of George Cabot Lodge* (Boston, 1911).

There are many biographies and monographs about Adams. The most complete biography is Ernest Samuels's three-volume work: *The Young Henry Adams* (Cambridge, Mass., 1948); *Henry Adams: The Middle Years* (Cambridge, Mass., 1958); *Henry Adams: The Major Phase* (Cambridge, Mass., 1964). A shorter but excellent biography is Elizabeth Stevenson's *Henry Adams* (New York, 1956). Even briefer is James Truslow Adams's readable *Henry Adams* (New York, 1933). Max I. Baym's *French Education of Henry Adams* (New York, 1951) is an account of his debt to French writers and thinkers.

Several monographs fall into the general category of literary criticism: John J. Conder, *A Formula All His Own* (Chicago, 1970); William Dusinberre, *Henry Adams, The Myth of Failure* (Charlottesville, Va., 1979); George Hochfield, *Henry Adams* (New York, 1962); Robert A. Hume, *Runaway Star* (Ithaca, N.Y., 1951); J. C. Levenson, *The Mind and Art of Henry Adams* (Stanford, Cal., 1957); Melvin Lyon, *Symbol and Idea in Henry Adams* (Lincoln, Neb., 1970); Robert Mane, *Henry Adams on the Road to Chartres* (Cambridge, Mass., 1971); James G. Murray, *Henry Adams* (New York, 1974); Vern Wagner, *The Suspension of Henry Adams* (Detroit, 1969).

Several studies concentrate on Adams as a historian: Timothy Paul Donovan, *Henry Adams and Brooks Adams* (Norman, Okla., 1961); Earl N. Harbert, *The Force So Much Closer Home* (New York, 1977); William Jordy, *Henry Adams, Scientific Historian* (New Haven, 1952). Although not wholly historiographical, Henry Wasser's *Scientific Thought of Henry Adams* (Thessaloniki, Greece, 1956) is helpful concerning Adams's theories of history. Ernest

Scheyer's *Circle of Henry Adams* (Detroit, 1970) deals with his artistic and literary friendships.

Many books treat the idea of the American experiment: R. L. Bruckberger, *Image of America* (New York, 1959); Michael Kammen, *People of Paradox* (New York, 1972); R. W. B. Lewis, *The American Adam* (Chicago, 1955); Frederick Merk, *Manifest Destiny and Mission in American History* (New York, 1963); Russel Nye, *This Almost Chosen People* (East Lansing, Mich., 1966); Max Silberschmidt, *The United States and Europe* (London, 1972); Henry Nash Smith, *Virgin Land* (Cambridge, Mass., 1950); Don M. Wolfe, *The Image of Man in America* (New York, 1970).

Helpful on Adams's Boston are these books: Russel B. Adams, Jr., *The Boston Money Tree* (New York, 1977); Cleveland Amory, *The Proper Bostonians* (New York, 1947); George Weston, *Boston Ways* (Boston, 1974).

The Adams family and its individual members are the subject of many works. On the family are these: James Truslow Adams, *The Adams Family* (New York, 1930); Francis Russell, *Adams, An American Dynasty* (New York, 1976); Jack Shepherd, *The Adams Chronicles* (Boston, 1975). For the fullest accounts of early family members, see Page Smith, *John Adams* (2 vols., Garden City, N.Y., 1962); Marie B. Hecht, *John Quincy Adams* (New York, 1972); Martin Duberman, *Charles Francis Adams* (Stanford, Cal., 1960). Henry's brother Brooks endeavored to assess the fourth generation's debts to the family heritage in his long introduction to *The Degradation of the Democratic Dogma* (New York, 1919). His brother Charles also considered the family influence in his *Autobiography* (Boston, 1916). Brooks and Charles are the subjects of revealing biographies: Thornton Anderson, *Brooks Adams* (Ithaca, N.Y., 1951); Arthur Beringause, *Brooks Adams* (New York, 1955); Edward C. Kirkland, *Charles Francis Adams, Jr.* (Cambridge, Mass., 1965). One of the nieces of the Adams brothers, Abigail Adams Homans, has written a charming memoir about them, *Education by Uncles* (Boston, 1966).

For the religious, educational, and intellectual milieu of Adams's childhood, see O. B. Frothingham, *Boston Unitarianism* (New York, 1890); Conrad Wright, *The Liberal Christians* (Boston, 1978); Frederick Rudolph, *The American College and Uni-*

versity (New York, 1962); Samuel Eliot Morison, *Three Centuries of Harvard* (Cambridge, Mass., 1936). Edward Lurie's *Louis Agassiz* (Chicago, 1960) not only elaborates scientific thinking during the mid-nineteenth century but also says much about Adams's Harvard.

Several volumes offer background on the years Adams spent as his father's private secretary: David M. Potter, *Lincoln and His Party in the Secession Crisis* (New Haven, 1942); William L. Burn, *The Age of Equipoise* (New York, 1964); Ephraim D. Adams, *Great Britain and the American Civil War* (New York, 1958); David P. Crook, *Diplomacy during the American Civil War* (New York, 1975).

Context for the political, economic, and intellectual influences on Adams while he was in England may be found in these books: Joseph Hamburger, *Intellectuals in Politics* (New Haven, 1965); Lloyd Kelley, *The Transatlantic Persuasion* (New York, 1969); George Morlan, *America's Heritage from John Stuart Mill* (New York, 1936); Henry Pelling, *America and the British Left* (New York, 1957); Marvin Zetterbaum, *Tocqueville and the Problem of Democracy* (Stanford, Cal., 1967); Kenneth Thompson, *Auguste Comte* (New York, 1975).

Helpful in appreciating the political atmosphere of the late 1860s and 1870s are these works: Matthew Josephson, *The Politicos* (New York, 1938); Howard Wayne Morgan, *From Hayes to McKinley* (Syracuse, N.Y., 1969); Howard Wayne Morgan (ed.), *The Gilded Age* (Syracuse, N.Y., 1970); William B. Hesseltine, *Ulysses S. Grant, Politician* (New York, 1935); Kenneth E. Davison, *The Presidency of Rutherford B. Hayes* (Westport, Conn., 1972); Allan Peskin, *Garfield, A Biography* (Kent, Ohio, 1978); David S. Mussey, *James G. Blaine* (New York, 1934). Equally important is a growing body of literature about the reformers of Adams's generation: Geoffrey Blodgett, *The Gentle Reformers* (Cambridge, Mass., 1966); John M. Dobson, *Politics in the Gilded Age* (New York, 1972); Gerald McFarlan, *Mugwumps, Morals, and Politics* (Amherst, Mass., 1975); Earle Dudley Ross, *The Liberal Republican Movement* (New York, 1971); John G. Sproat, *The Best Men* (New York, 1968).

On Adams's years as Harvard professor see Samuel Eliot Morison (ed.), *The Development of Harvard College since the Inaugu-*

ration of President Eliot (Cambridge, Mass., 1930); Hugh Hawkins, *Between Harvard and America: The Educational Leadership of Charles William Eliot* (New York, 1972); Charles William Eliot, *Educational Reform* (New York, 1898).

The flavor of Adams's social life in Washington is presented in the *Letters of Mrs. Henry Adams,* edited by Ward Thoron (Boston, 1936) and in *Clover* by Otto Friedrich (New York, 1979). The state of historical research and writing when Adams undertook his histories is treated in Herbert Baxter Adams's *Historical Scholarship in the United States, 1876–1901* (Baltimore, 1938), and in Richard Vitzthum's *The American Compromise* (Norman, Okla., 1974).

Adams's *History* is more understandable in light of recent studies of the Jefferson and Madison years. Valuable are these works: Noble E. Cunningham, *The Jeffersonian Republicans in Power* (Chapel Hill, N.C., 1963); Ralph Ketcham, *James Madison* (New York, 1971); Adrienne Koch, *Jefferson and Madison* (New York, 1950); Merrill Peterson, *The Jeffersonian Image in the American Mind* (New York, 1960) and *Thomas Jefferson and the New Nation* (New York, 1970); Leonard P. White, *The Jeffersonians* (New York, 1951); Charles M. Wiltse, *The Jeffersonian Tradition in American Democracy* (New York, 1960). There is also William Henry Smith's telling criticism, *A Case of Hereditary Bias: Henry Adams as an Historian* (New York, 1890).

Adams's unhappiness with the United States in the 1890s is illuminated by several studies of the period: Edward C. Kirkland, *Industry Comes of Age* (New York, 1961); W. J. Lauck, *Causes of the Panic of 1893* (Boston, 1907); Stanley L. Jones, *The Presidential Election of 1896* (Madison, Wis., 1964); Margaret Leech, *In the Days of McKinley* (New York, 1959). Adams's anti-Semitism and class biases make more sense within the context of E. Digby Baltzell's *Protestant Establishment* (New York, 1964) and Stow Persons's *Decline of American Gentility* (New York, 1973).

Works dealing with the Spanish-American War and its consequences are these: Robert L. Beisner, *Twelve Against Empire* (New York, 1968); Howard Wayne Morgan, *America's Road to Empire* (New York, 1965). Kenton J. Clymer's *John Hay* (Ann Arbor, Mich., 1975) is an excellent biography of Adams's diplomat friend.

On American expatriots see Ishbel Ross's *The Expatriots* (New York, 1970). There is no good work of a general nature on the *fin de siècle*. Two contemporary pieces are informative: James Arthur Balfour, *Decadence* (Cambridge, Eng., 1908), and Max Nordau, *Degeneration* (New York, 1895). Helpful, too, are Van Wyck Brooks's *America's Coming of Age* (Garden City, N.Y., 1958) and John Milner's *Symbolists and Decadents* (New York, 1971).

William O'Neill's *Woman Movement* (Chicago, 1971) lends perspective to Adams and feminism. Adams's view of the Virgin as earth goddess is reinforced in Robert Graves's *The White Goddess* (New York, 1966) and Marina Warner's *Alone of All Her Sex: The Myth and the Cult of the Virgin Mary* (New York, 1976).

Adams's theories of history owed much to his age's understanding of evolution. See Robert Bannister, *Social Darwinism: Science and Myth in Anglo-American Social Thought* (Philadelphia, 1979); Paul A. Carter, *The Spiritual Crisis of the Gilded Age* (DeKalb, Ill., 1971); G. S. Carver, *A Hundred Years of Evolution* (New York, 1957); Richard Hofstadter, *Social Darwinism in American Thought* (Philadelphia, 1944); Frank Marsh, *Evolution, Creation, and Science* (Washington, D.C., 1944). Also concerning the thought of the period are Henry F. May's *The End of American Innocence* (New York, 1959) and Vernon L. Parrington's *The Beginnings of Critical Realism in America* (New York, 1930).

Acknowledgments

MY EARLIEST DEBTS are to former professors at Miami University, to Harris Warren, who introduced Adams over a decade ago, and to Robert Reid, who directed my first large study of Adams. Colleague John Lukacs read and criticized the entire manuscript and was helpful throughout. Others at Chestnut Hill College made much appreciated corrections and observations: Les Conner, James Sullivan, and Joanna Myers. My uncle Perrin Hazelton offered valuable insights from his vantage as former editor and thoughtful reader. Thanks are also due the Massachusetts Historical Society for permitting use of the Adams Papers and to Helen Hayes, reference librarian at Chestnut Hill's Logue Library.

I am especially grateful to Oscar Handlin, who gave me a chance to write for the Library of American Biography and who skillfully pared my excesses. Little, Brown's Marian Ferguson never lost faith and spurred me on at the darkest moments. I am also indebted to my skilled and exacting copyeditor Carol Beal as well as to Elizabeth M. Schaaf and Mary E. Tondorf-Dick, both of the Little, Brown editorial staff. Finally, my wife Jessica was an inspiring partner, from initial discussions to final rewriting. Indeed, the book's organization is largely hers.

Index